PORTRAITS

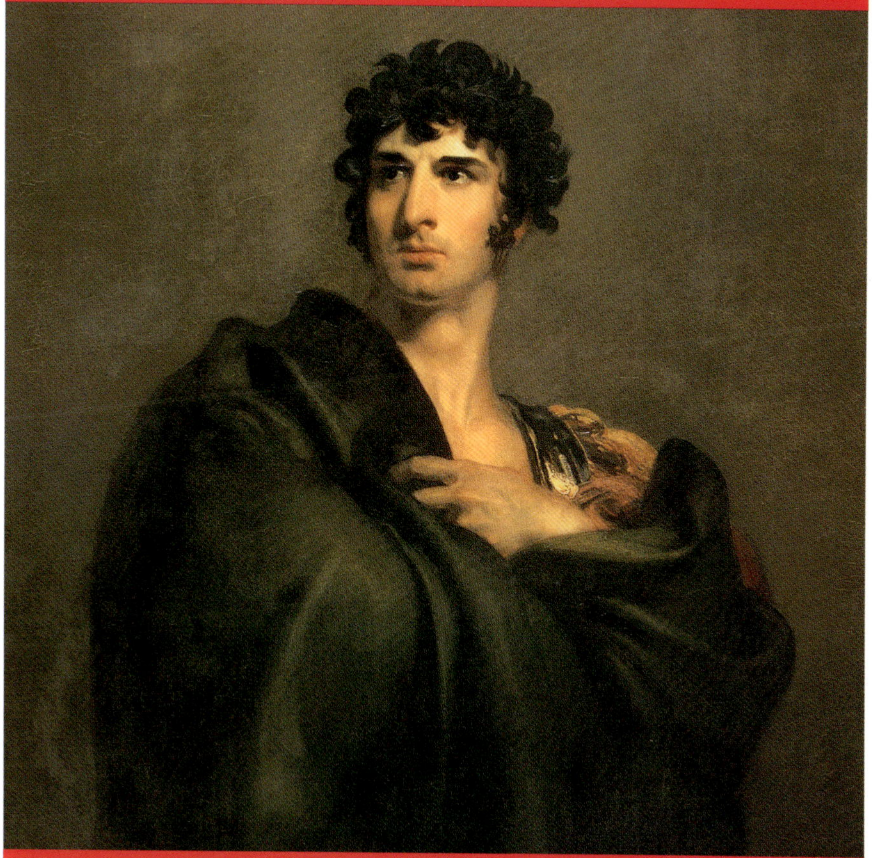

GUILDHALL ART GALLERY

ACKNOWLEDGEMENTS

This book was written by Vivien Knight, who is grateful to the following: Guildhall Library; Corporation of London Records Office; Denbighshire Record Office; North Yorkshire Record Office; Timothy Duke, Chester Herald, College of Arms; Librarian of the Worshipful Company of Goldsmiths; Sinéad McCoole. Jackie Lea and Naomi Allen liaised with the designer and producer. Naomi Allen undertook the editorial and proofreading work and obtained the photographic materials for illustrations and Jeremy Johnson arranged new photography. References in the text to the IGI are to the International Genealogical Index – part of Family Search, compiled by the Church of Jesus Christ of Latter-day Saints from parish registers and other sources.

ISBN 1-902795-04-0

Cover: John Michael Wright *Sir John Robinson* (p. 23)
Title page: Sir Thomas Lawrence (detail) *John Philip Kemble as Coriolanus* (p. 46)
Back cover: Sir John Lavery (detail) *Portrait of Lady Lavery* (p. 63)
Photographs courtesy of Bridgeman Art Library

Published by Guildhall Art Gallery, 1999
Designed by Mick Keates
Produced by Supreme Publishing Services

PORTRAIT PAINTING IN ENGLAND originated in altarpieces and other religious subjects but had become an art form in its own right by the sixteenth century. Apart from decorative work it was the only form of painting allowed after 1535 when Henry VIII suppressed religious subject matter. Cultured and accomplished, Henry was an important patron of the arts and foreign artists drawn to his court – of whom Holbein is the best known – exerted a strong influence on native portrait painters. The portrait of Sir Thomas Exmewe, Lord Mayor in 1517 (page 8) was believed to be by Holbein when it was presented to the Corporation in 1919, but it has since been attributed to the English painter John Bettes, thought on stylistic grounds possibly to have worked in his studio. In the seventeenth century immigrant artists from Northern Europe dominated portrait painting in England and it was not until the following century that a wholly British school of portrait painting was established, with Hogarth, Reynolds and Gainsborough its best known practitioners. Even after the introduction of landscape painting in the second half of the seventeenth century, portraiture remained the most important and flourishing form of art in England until at least Victorian times.

There are no records of paintings in Guildhall before 1670 although in 1607 a John Cobbold was 'made free of this City by redemption in the Company of Painter-Stainers' on condition that 'he first give to the City the Kings Majesty's Picture in a fair table, to remain with the Lord Mayor for the time being'. There are no further references to this or any other picture in the Corporation's records until in 1670 the Court of Aldermen resolved to commission portraits of the judges appointed to settle property claims in the wake of the Great Fire of London, 'to be taken by a skillful hand & kept in some public place of the Citty for a gratefull memoriall of this good office'. Four artists were recommended to the Court: Peter Lely (born in Westphalia and the favourite painter of the Restoration Court) and Jacob Huysmans (from Antwerp), and the Englishmen John Michael Wright and John Hayles. A committee was appointed to 'informe themselves & consider which one or more of the said Masters to employ in that worke & make agreement with him or them for doing the same accordingly with all convenient speed'. According to George Vertue, they would have chosen Lely, 'but he would not wait upon the Judges in the City to paint them wherefore Wright had them to do.' One of the Committee members was Sir John Robinson, whom Wright had painted seven years earlier (page 23); he was also later to be employed by another member, Sir Robert Vyner. Wright had completed fourteen judges' portraits at £36 each by the end of 1671; eight more portraits were added to the series up to 1675. The diarist John Evelyn saw those already hung in 1673 and wrote, 'most of them are very like the Persons they are made to represent, though I never took Write to be any considerable artist.' Painted as speedily as they were and all depicted front view in similar robes, the Judges' portraits had none of the implied movement of Wright's earlier portrait of Sir John Robinson or the kind of individual characterisation that marks Robinson's coarse and aggressive features. Instead the artist employed strong centralised images which derived their power from repetition; some idea of their imposing grandeur as a series is offered by William Miller's *Oath to Alderman Newnham* (page 37).

The Fire Judges' portraits were hung in Guildhall, the lower part of the windows being blocked up to accommodate them, and over the next century they were joined by portraits which the Corporation commissioned to express its loyalty to the Crown and to honour its friends. In September 1670 the Court of Aldermen commissioned Lely to paint Charles II and James, Duke of York 'as some remembrance of their Royall Favoures and encouragements to the worke of rebuilding the Citty' and paid him £100 for the two portraits in December 1671. The Duke of York's picture was slashed across the legs in 1681; a reward of £500 was offered and a suspect examined but exonerated. A portrait of William III hanging in Guildhall was slashed in November 1689 and the Court again offered a £500 reward. The picture had not yet been paid for and it was not until the following April that Richard Haines, Citizen and Painter, was paid £30 for the portraits of William III and Queen Mary, since identified as being by Jan van der Vaardt, a Dutch immigrant who had begun his career as a drapery painter. The Aldermen had been considering commissioning the German artist Sir Godfrey Kneller to paint the King and paying him out of their own pockets, but nothing seems to have come of this. In 1701 Kneller was one of five artists asked to submit designs for a portrait of Queen Anne in her coronation robes but it was another German artist, John Closterman (1660-1711), who was successful and was paid £100 for it the following year.

By the time Kneller next came into contact with the Corporation he was the most prosperous and important portrait painter in England. The Court of Common Council had decided in May 1716 to put up a painting of George I and the King said he would send for Kneller, his Principal Painter. Kneller did not appear at Guildhall until January 1717, when he measured the portrait of Queen Anne and said that the King's picture should be the same size. The portrait was still not ready by March 1718, when the Court sent a warrant requiring him to deliver it. When Sir Robert Child reported on September 23 that he had seen the finished picture at Kneller's studio, the Lord Mayor wrote to the artist instructing him to deliver the picture before the following Monday when there was to be 'a General Meeting of the Citizens of London in Common Hall.' Kneller's reply made it clear that he alone would decide when the picture was to be delivered, and also reveals the practical difficulties involved: 'My Lord, I had the Honour of having your Lordship's letter, and shoud have Sent His Majesty's picture, to be put up, on Monday, if it weare Dry Enough, for the Longer it stays it will be better. I promised, Sr Robbert Chyld when with me heer I woud come to London in a forthnight's time and see how best so Large a picture might be placed and which should be on the Cornish [cornice] of the Whenscoat [wainscoting]; and so should the Queens &c, which picture is now [hung?] higher. I have ordered a board, for to be behind the King's picture, and which shall be up in less than a fourthnight Time. And the picture being as large as the Queens, 12 foot high and 8 foot wyde it must be roled, caried to the Hall, and be strayned [i.e. stretched] ther and Set up in an after noon, when the Hall is Empty of any people; the scaffolding, should be reddy before. I will wrigt to Mr Strasey [Sir Randolph Stracey, the Town Clerk] some days before when I intend to be at the Hall, and will appoint the day for setting it up, and am My Lord your Lordships Most obedient Humble Servent G Kneller.'

The portraits in Guildhall had already been cleaned or 'refreshed' (repainted?) several times by 1727, when they were cleaned again and the hall was ordered to be 'beautified' for the reception of two new portraits of George II and Queen Caroline by Kneller's former pupil and his successor as Principal Painter, the Irish artist Charles Jervas (c.1675-1739); Closterman's portrait of Queen Anne and Kneller's of George I were now cut down to match them in size. Portraits of King George III and Queen Charlotte in their coronation robes were presented by the King in 1764, the Corporation having requested him to sit for his portrait three years before. They were copies of an original pair painted in 1761 by Allan Ramsay, who had to employ assistants to meet the great demand for replicas of them; his studio was so successful that he was able to retire from painting in the mid-1760s. Portrait painters employed assistants from at least the seventeenth century and the most fashionable and successful operated what was almost a factory system, whereby the artist painted only the faces and his assistants undertook most of the rest, with specialist drapery painters doing the garments – not always the sitter's own – which were brought to the studio to be painted, the artist providing the finishing overall touches that unified the work. In February 1764 the Court of Common Council had commissioned Joshua Reynolds to paint the full length portrait of Sir Charles Pratt, Lord Chief Justice of the Common Pleas, in gratitude for his ruling against the imprisonment of Alderman John Wilkes in the Tower, but because the drapery and background were believed to be painted by assistants in 1968 it was decided that instead of restoring the damaged bottom part the picture should be cut down.

Reynolds's portrait of Pratt had a history of flaking and had been returned to the artist for repair as early as 1777. It had hung with the rest of the Corporation's portraits in the Guildhall, which is known to have been damp and smoky. In 1778 the Corporation's surveyor George Dance reported that Kneller's portrait of George I was 'so much decayed and torn as not to be capable of repair', while in 1779 all the pictures – now removed from the Guildhall, which was being refurbished, to the neighbouring Guildhall Chapel – were in a 'dirty condition and some by age and dampness totally destroyed.' From several restorers who had supplied estimates the Corporation chose Spiridione Roma, who like other restorers of the time was a painter. By July 1780 he had 'cleaned, repaired and perfectly restored' nineteen of the Judges' portraits, and seven of the royal portraits ('six of whom was entirely destroyed') together with Kneller's portrait of George I ('being many score of small pieces put together again and completely reduced to one'). Roma's cleaning process was described in an obituary as 'dissolving the varnish and dirt which adhered to the painting [...] which he removed with a small ivory scraper without any injury to the body of colour on the canvas'; unfortunately his treatment of the Fire Judges seems to have included scouring off much of Wright's original surface to provide a tooth for his own overpainting. When the greenish-black background overpaint was partially removed from the portrait of Sir Matthew Hale several years ago it revealed the ghostly remains of a shallow architectural setting with a balustrade and steps; perhaps the dirt and smoke in the Guildhall had obliterated these details for so long that no-one noticed their loss at Roma's hands.

Closterman's portrait of Queen Anne and both of Lely's paintings of Charles II and the Duke of York had disappeared by at least 1827. Kneller's portrait of George I survived until December 29 1940, when it was lost in the air raid that burnt the Guildhall and destroyed the Common Council Chamber and its Lobby, where the picture then hung. The 'Fire Judges' hung in Guildhall Art Gallery from 1909 but were taken down and stored in the Crypts beneath Guildhall during the Second World War. There they were soaked by the water used to extinguish the fires above on the night of December 29 1940, bringing with it chalk washed from the mediaeval foundations of the Guildhall. Torn, blistered and peeling, they were considered too difficult or even impossible to repair and in 1952 the Court of Common Council decided to dispose of all but two. Offered first to the National Portrait Gallery and other collections, eventually thirteen were presented to interested bodies or individuals and seven identified as beyond repair were given to the Courtauld Institute for research.

In view of the poor condition of the Guildhall's portraits in 1779 it is not surprising that henceforth only sculptures – considered to be more durable – were commissioned for Guildhall: a monument commemorating William Beckford had been erected in 1770, and Bacon's monument to the Earl of Chatham, commissioned in 1779, was completed in 1783. In that year the Court of Common Council decided to commemorate the popular British victory over the Spanish at Gibraltar in September 1782 with a painting for the Common Council Chamber, and gave the commission to the expatriate American artist John Singleton Copley. Finally hung in the Chamber in 1795, his painting *The Defeat of the Floating Batteries* (also known as *The Siege of Gibraltar*) contains life-size portraits of the officers of the Gibraltar garrison, seen defending the colony under the direction of General Sir George Augustus Elliott (Lord Heathfield). Although his reputation in England now rests largely on his 'modern history' paintings like this one, Copley made his living largely as a portrait painter. In 1794 Alderman John Boydell commissioned him to paint the portrait of Marquis Cornwallis (page 40), one of eight distinguished naval and military commanders whose portraits Boydell presented as part of a larger scheme for display in the

Common Council Chamber between 1792 and 1801. Among them was a portrait of Lord Heathfield commissioned from Sir Joshua Reynolds ('the most Capital Portrait ever Painted by this Master'), which his nephew Josiah Boydell removed from the Chamber after the Alderman's death in 1804 (apparently because it was hanging on a damp wall) and with the Court's agreement substituted a copy. The picture was sold to Sir Thomas Lawrence in 1809 and is now in the National Gallery. (Northcote's portrait of Lord Howe was also replaced with a substitute – by G Kirtland – as the original had decayed.) When the Court of Common Council asked Alderman Boydell in 1800 to sit for his portrait he chose to be painted as Lord Mayor although it was ten years since his mayoralty (page 48). This is one of only two portraits of Lord Mayors in their robes to have been commissioned by the Corporation (the other is Richard Stone's portrait of Dame Mary Donaldson, commissioned in 1985 to commemorate the first female Lord Mayor of London). In the nineteenth century most of the Corporation's portrait commissions consisted of marble busts, although an important exception was the portrait of Richard Clark commissioned from Sir Thomas Lawrence in 1825 as a mark of respect for Clark's character and the service he had rendered the City as Lord Mayor in 1784 and Chamberlain from 1798. This was followed by Sir George Hayter's portrait of Queen Victoria enthroned in the House of Lords, which the Queen presented to the Corporation in 1839, following its request to her two years earlier to sit for her portrait.

Today Guildhall Art Gallery is probably best known for its Victorian paintings and its London subjects, but the Corporation's portraits remain a substantial and important part of its collection. The portrait of *Sir Thomas Exmewe* (page 8) painted c.1517 is currently the earliest example while the portrait of former Recorder Sir Lawrence Verney was completed to a commission of the Court of Aldermen as this introduction was being written in February 1999. Sitters range from Sir Thomas Lawrence's dramatic characterisation of the actor John Philip Kemble in role as Coriolanus (page 46) to the socialite Hazel Lavery, painted by her husband Sir John Lavery in 1922 (page 63). In recent years the Gallery has purchased portraits of modest Londoners like Sergeant Bert Bowers, a Chelsea Pensioner painted by Leonard McComb in 1992 (illustrated in *Modern Pictures*) as well as that of the wealthy Sir William Craven, Lord Mayor in 1610 (page 13). After the Greater London Council was disbanded, its own collection of portraits of the chairmen of the LCC and GLC was transferred to the Corporation's care in 1989 as a valuable document of London's history, bringing with it not only older establishment names like Sargent and Lavery but works by Peter Greenham and Maggi Hambling among many others.

ATTRIBUTED TO JOHN BETTES fl. c.1531-c.1570

Sir Thomas Exmewe, Lord Mayor 1517

oil on panel

Presented by the Hon. Mrs. Laurence Brodrick, 1919

Sir Thomas Exmewe was born about 1454 in Ruthin, Flintshire, the son of a prosperous Anglo-Norman mercer. He was apprenticed to London goldsmith Richard Burton in 1468 and became a freeman of the Goldsmiths' Company ten years later, being elected to the Livery in 1485. Exmewe had at least nine apprentices of his own from 1483 onwards and became Renter (junior) Warden of the Goldsmiths' Company in 1487.

Edward IV had given the Goldsmiths' Company the privilege of inspecting and regulating all gold and silver wares throughout the Kingdom, and the power to punish offenders for working or selling adulterated material. Their assay-wardens travelled the country for this purpose, and in 1490 Exmewe was fined 20 shillings for putting out the making of two salts and sending a dozen spoons to the burnishers, both many dwt (pennyweight) below the standard of sterling. He had also taken to sell at Stourbridge Fair a gilt cup 20 dwt below sterling, and when detected he had exhibited 'ungodly demeanour and language.' These transgressions appear to have been no impediment to his ascent through the ranks of the Company, and he was Warden in 1491 and 1499 and Prime Warden six times between 1507 and 1528.

Exmewe was an auditor to the City Corporation from 1503 to 1505 and again between 1515 and 1517. He was elected Sheriff in 1508 and also Alderman of Cripplegate Ward (which he held until his death in February 1529). In May 1509 he was one of the many granted a general pardon by the new King Henry VIII, although the nature of his offence is unknown; later he is recorded as a supplier to the Court, and in 1512 he was a member of a commission inquiring in London and Middlesex into extortions and deceptions by goldsmiths Robert Fenrother (Alderman for Aldgate Ward 1511-24 and Sheriff 1512-13) and Will Rede, who had been joint Masters of the Mint of Henry VII in the Tower of London. Exmewe was elected Lord Mayor in 1517 and was knighted on March 20 1518 at a great feast given by the Bishop of Durham at his house in the Strand to the King, Cardinal Wolsey and other dignitaries. An important act of charity early in Exmewe's mayoralty in January 1518 was, as John Stow recorded, to 'breke the wall of this citie besyde the Moregate and there to make a Conduyte at his own costs and charges for the conveying of the water from the Manor of Fynesbury and then to make up the seyd wall again'. (Exmewe borrowed the lead to make this fresh water conduit, at the junction of London Wall and Coleman Street, from the City's store. It was not until nine years later

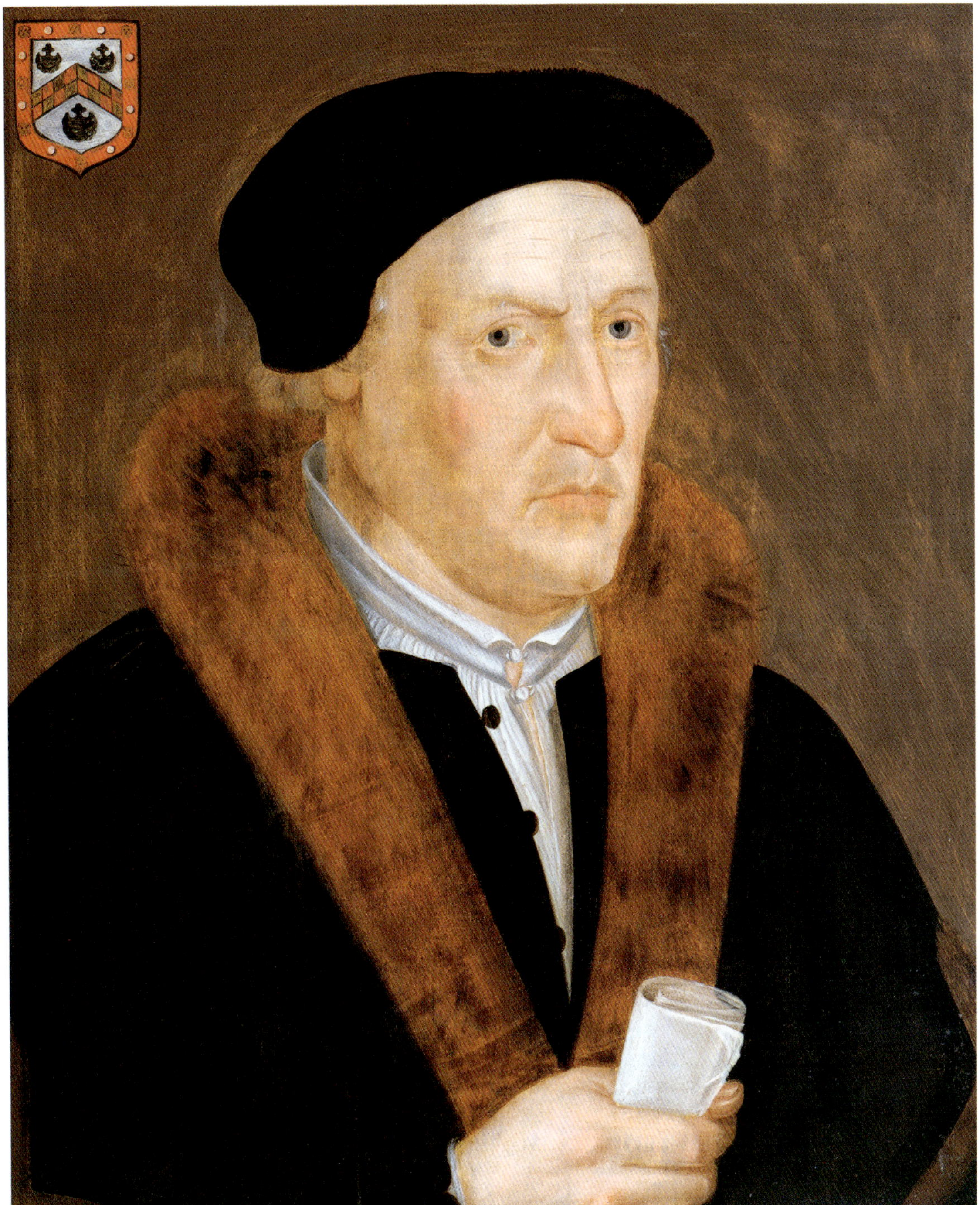

that the Chamberlain ordered him to replace it but, by this time old and probably ill, Exmewe preferred to reimburse the City's purse instead.) In July Cardinal Campeggio came as papal legate to see the King, his procession stretching two miles along streets jammed with cheering crowds, and when he reached Cheapside he was received by the Lord Mayor and Aldermen in their best liveries, and Sir Thomas More (who was Under-sheriff between 1510 and 1519) gave an address in Latin on behalf of the city. Later in his mayoral year Exmewe held a 'costly dinner' at Goldsmiths' Hall for the French ambassadors sent by Francis I to King Henry VIII, 'which dinner they highly praysed, it was so well ordered.' He was a Commissioner of the Peace for the County of Middlesex in 1518 and for several subsequent years until 1526, and for the County of Surrey in 1520 and 1522.

Exmewe died on February 6 1529 and was buried in a chapel in the church of St Mary Magdalene in Milk Street (burnt in the Great Fire of 1666). Aldermen who were past the Chair (i.e. who had been Lord Mayor) were traditionally buried at night with great ceremony, and the instructions Exmewe gave in his main will show that he envisaged the custom being followed at his own burial. He made three wills, the first dated December 17 1528 in which he left a tenement in Hogenlane to the Master and Wardens of the Haberdashers' Company, charging them with the observance of an obit (a yearly remembrance on the anniversary of the person's death) for the soul of John Mathew, late Yeoman of the Chamber to King Henry VII, citizen and baker, his wife Katherine and others. A copy of another dated 24 January 1529 is in the Goldsmiths' Company's Register of Deeds and deals with an annuity of £7.6.8 from the church of St Thomas of Acon, which he bequeathed to the Goldsmiths on condition they used it to provide a priest for St Mary Magdalene Milk Street and an obit. Exmewe's main will dated January 6 1529 left legacies to the wife and children of his friend and executor Thomas Kytson, as well as £50 to provide and purchase lands and 'tenements' to provide an income for his own daughter Elizabeth, a nun at the convent of the Virgin Mary and St Margaret, Dartford, and after her death to be used to provide a yearly obit. (The convent was suppressed in 1536 and Elizabeth moved to the Shrine of Our Lady of Walsingham in Norfolk.) His legacies and the language in which they were couched marking him as a devout Catholic, Exmewe also left money to the priests of St Augustine on the Wall (also known as St Augustine Papey) St Mary Axe, of which he stated he was 'a brother', on condition they attended his funeral and prayed for his soul.

Exmewe's wife Elizabeth had been married before and already had a son and two daughters, the latter of whom, together with their own sons, were beneficiaries in Exmewe's will of January 6. Exmewe left nothing to his step-son, John West, an Observant

Friar and one of Wolsey's secret agents, and West complained to Wolsey that Exmewe had witheld from him and his sister Katharine 'certain evidences of lands in Middlesex which I sold her and her husband William at the death of my mother Lady Elizabeth Exmew [sic] who died 14 Feb 1528. He also witheld from my sister 20*l*. ster., also a chalice and vestment, a chain of gold of 42oz., 6 rings of gold set with stones and 5*l*.6*s*.8*d*. bequeathed me by Wm Browne, late Alderman of London. My father-in-law [sic] Exmew promised that my sister and her husband should be his executors; but his executors Th. Kytson, mercer, and one Broket, goldsmith, retain all his goods.'

In March 1519 Exmewe had sold his old family home in Ruthin to a prosperous local Anglo-Norman mercer, Edward Goodman (d.1560). Exmewe House was a fourteenth-century timber framed building occupying a commanding position on St Peter's Square (it was demolished in 1928 and replaced by a Barclay's Bank), and Goodman may have occupied it as his business address while continuing to live at neighbouring Nantclwyd House. One of his three sons, Gawen Goodman, mentioned Exmewe's portrait in his will (1627) together with his own portrait and that of his father as 'being now in the parlor of the house wherein I now dwell. And my will is that the said pictures should remaine in the said parlor' – presumed to be in either Exmewe House or Nantclwyd House. Although the Goodman family also had a London connection and could thus have obtained the painting at any time before Gawen Goodman's death (his brother Gabriel was Dean of Westminster and his son was buried in the cloister of Westminster Abbey in 1576), it has traditionally been assumed that the portrait was already hanging in Exmewe House when it was sold, and thus must have been painted before 1519.

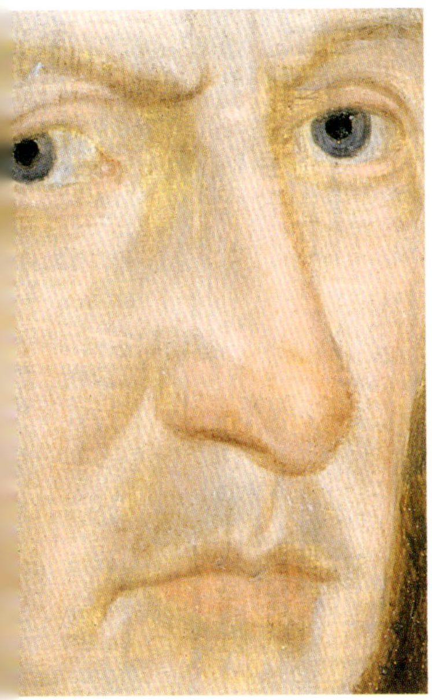

Following the marriage of Gawen Goodman's descendant Jane Goodman to Meredydd Wynne of Coedcoch, Abergele about 1700, the portrait passed down the Wynne family to Major General E W Lloyd Wynne. It was his widow (by then both remarried and widowed a second time) who presented it to the Corporation of London at a meeting of the Court of Common Council in November 1919. The Court resolved unanimously 'that the best thanks of this Court be and are hereby tendered to the Hon. Mrs Laurence Brodrick for her generous and valuable gift [...] which this court receives with much gratitude and will place with their other works of art, ever to be kept as one of their most treasured possessions and as a record of the generosity of the donor', and passed it to the Director of Guildhall Art Gallery, Alfred Temple: on December 1 he reported that the picture had been hung.

Exmewe's portrait is one of singular power and characterisation, even though its paint is now very worn and thin. Despite the sitter's ascetic and severe appearance, his wealth is shown by his fur stole, and the armholes of his gown are also edged with fur: English sumptuary laws forbad the wearing of fur to everyone below the rank of knight so this may indicate that the picture was painted after he was Lord Mayor. In Exmewe's coat of arms the leopards' faces allude to the London assay mark and thus to his trade as a goldsmith, while the plates may refer to silver coin. It has been suggested that the escallops may refer to trade overseas, and as his friend Sir Thomas Kytson was a Merchant Adventurer perhaps Exmewe too engaged in foreign trade; this would account for the expensive and at that time rare Turkey carpet which is mentioned in his will, as well as offering the possibility that his portrait could have been painted abroad (his fur-edged gown is virtually identical to the one worn by Petrus Aegidius in the portrait of 1517 by the Flemish master Quentin Massys). When the portrait was presented in 1919 it was attributed to Holbein, who paid his first visit to England in 1526-1528, staying with Sir Thomas More in Chelsea. Exmewe must have known More through their official duties and could through him have come into contact with Holbein, especially as his friend Kytson also had his portrait painted by the artist. (In 1526, however, Exmewe would have been about seventy-two years old – somewhat older perhaps than his apparent age in this portrait). Before having a plaque bearing Holbein's name made for the picture Temple requested permission 'to obtain an opinion from one of the eminent authorities on the continent, should he be visiting London. While their fees are high for opinions of this kind, I have no doubt I could obtain one for a nominal fee of five guineas.' On April 23 1923 Temple reported that he had paid the eminent Dutch art historian Hofstede de Groot five guineas to inspect the portrait at the Gallery, informing the Library Committee: 'He is quite certain it is not by Holbein, but regards it as a very interesting picture in excellent condition, and a genuine work of the Holbein period, probably by John Bettes who lived in Holbein's time and died in 1570, so I think it would be justifiable to ascribe the picture as painted by Bettes – as Mr Cust, the King's Surveyor of Pictures, is also inclined to ascribe the work to him.' Bettes is one of the few native English artists whose names are recorded and who is thought from his manner possibly to have worked in Holbein's studio. The identification of Exmewe's portrait as his work seems to rest largely on its similarity to Bettes' *Unknown Man* in the Tate Gallery. This – signed in French *faict par jehan Bettes Anglois* – is dated 1545 and his other known works also date from around this period, which – taken in conjunction with his supposed date of death – would suggest that Exmewe's portrait would have to have been an early work.

Attributed to **Marcus Gheeraerts the Younger** 1561-1635

Sir William Craven, Lord Mayor 1610

oil on canvas
Purchased, 1991

William Craven's parents came from the village of Appletreewick in the parish of Burnsall in Yorkshire. They may have lived for a while in London – which attracted immigrants from all over the country – since his birth appears in the IGI to be recorded there 'about 1548' together with that of his older brother Henry (1543-1603). An existing connection would explain why in 1562 his parents sent the fourteen-year-old William from Appletreewick to London with a common carrier to be apprenticed to Robert Hulson, a mercer and draper of Watling Street in the parish of St John the Evangelist. Hulson was a man of established position in the Merchant Taylors' Company and its Master in 1569, when Craven's term of apprenticeship ended and he obtained his Freedom. Craven had lived with Hulson during his apprenticeship and now became tenant of a shop owned by him. However in 1582 they quarrelled and took the matter to the Master and Wardens of the Merchant Taylors for arbitration. The dispute was settled and the tenancy ended by Hulson paying £10 to Craven and having his shop back for his own use. The following year Craven was elected to the livery of the Company on the payment of a £1 fine. About this time he leased a house in the parish of St Antholin's from the Mercers' Company where he both resided and carried on business in partnership with two fellow Merchant Taylors, John and Robert Parker (who may have been related to him and to whom he left the house in his will).

Craven was elected Warden of the Merchant Taylors' Company in 1593 when, as John Stow recorded, the plague was 'hot in the city' and, the Lord Mayor having prohibited any such assemblies, instead of the the customary election dinner the cost of it went towards the charitable relief of victims. The following year he was elected to the Court of Assistants in recognition of his service to the Company, having contributed £20 in March 1593 towards the building of widows' almshouses in Hog Lane and then making a weekly payment of 16d, the cost of maintaining one widow, for the rest of her life. Craven was elected Alderman for Bishopsgate Ward in April 1600 and in June he became Sheriff. As was customary, the Company voted him £30 towards his shrieval expences and lent him their plate for his inaugural banquet. In 1602 he became Alderman of Cordwainer Ward and in the following year he was knighted by James I.

When Craven became Lord Mayor in 1610 the Merchant Taylors' Company voted 100 marks 'towards the trimmings of his Ldship's house'. The traditional Lord Mayor's

Procession had been abandoned for some time but was now revived by order of the King, and the Company prepared a costly show of great splendour to honour their liveryman as he went to take his oath before the Barons of the Exchequer at Westminster. The Company's accounts reveal that the procession cost £805.4s.5d and included pageants of a ship with guns, three lions, two unicorns, a camel and two giants as well as one of Merlin sitting on a rock in the Thames, while payments are listed for a variety of services from the painting and gilding of banners, to hundreds of new gowns and other apparel and breakfasts provided in Blackwell Hall for all the children enlisted to appear in the procession. Until 1751, when the calendar was reformed by the omission of eleven days, the Lord Mayor Elect was admitted into office on the Feast of SS Simon and Jude, October 28, and processed to Westminster the following day. October 29 1610 coincided with the state visit of Christian of Anhalt who, according to Howe's *Chronicles*, 'survayed the cittie of London with great pleasure and admiration, and behelde the pleasant triumphs upon the water, and within the cittie, which at this time were extraordinary, in honor of the lord maior and citizens; and that day this prince, with all his Germayne trayne, were entertained at the lord maior's feast in the Guildhall; where he manifested his former admiration, touching the greatnesse, situation, state, and wealth of the cittie, and then he observed and admired the goodly uniforme, order and rich habite of the citizens; and sayd there was no cittie nor state in the world that did elect their magistrates with such magnificence, except the cittie of Venice, unto which the cittie of London commeth very neere.'

Wool and cloth were England's most significant exports at this time and like others involved in this trade Craven was by now a wealthy man. Although he presumably remained in the cloth trade until 1617, when he gave up the tenter grounds which he had leased from the Merchant Taylors' Company for the past eleven years, he was involved with the East India Company from at least 1609: in 1614 he lent it money, and a year later he was one of those appointed by the Crown to examine those 'suspected persons that intend interloping into the East Indies or Muscovy' – i.e. threatening the Company's monopoly – and to bind over those they found culpable to appear before the Privy Council. But Craven is also remembered for the exceptional degree of his charitable activities. He maintained close connections with his native parish of Burnsall, where his family still lived, and as well as building or restoring three stone bridges in the neighbourhood and paving the highways between Burnsall and Appletreewick, in 1602 he built a grammar school there for the education of poor children (the building was extended in 1966 and is still in use as Burnsall Primary School). In 1604 he was involved in a scheme to establish 'a new college after the manner of a university' at Ripon in Yorkshire and in 1612 his improvements to

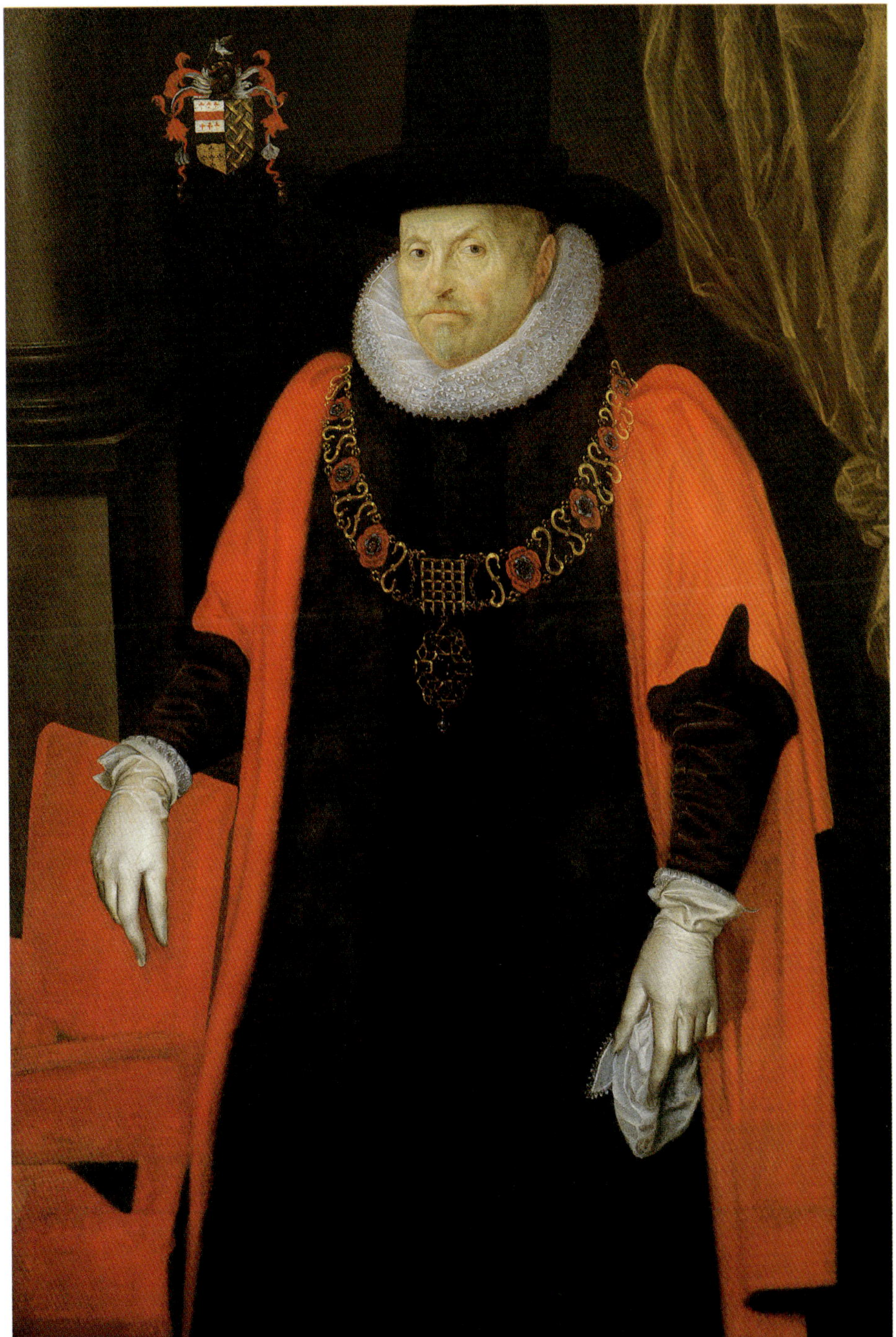

the parish church at Burnsall included new seats and repairs which were commemorated with this verse inscribed in the choir:

'This church of beauty most repaired thus so bright
Two hundred Pounds did cost Sir William Craven Knighte
Many other Workes of Charitie, whereof no mention here
True Tokens of his Bountie in this Parish did appeare
The Place of his Nativitie in Appletrewick is seene
And late of London Citie, Lord Mayor hee hathe beene
The Care of this Worke soe beautiful and faire
Was put to John Topham Clerke by the late Lord Mayor
Of that most famous Citie of London so brighte
By Sir William Craven that bountiful Knighte
Borne in this Parish at Appletrewick Towne
Who regarded no Cost so the Worke was well done.

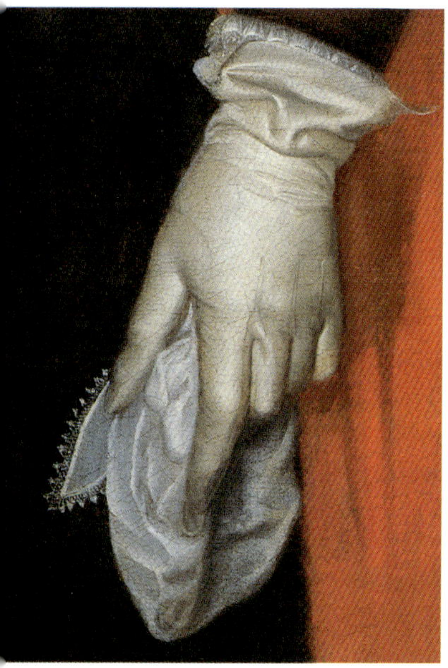

Craven was elected President of Christ's Hospital in 1611 and shortly afterwards gave it £1000 to purchase the advowson, or living, of Ugley in Essex and the right to present it. He had given £50 in 1596 towards the building of St John's College, Oxford, with which the Merchant Taylors had a connection through their school in St Lawrence Pountney, while in 1605 he had been part of a deputation to the Bishop of Winchester in connection with a controversy over the College's rejection of poor scholars. In order to encourage the study of Divinity and to provide a living to which students could be preferred, in 1613 Craven purchased the living of Creeke in Northamptonshire and conveyed it to the College, with the intention that it be filled by one of the school's former pupils. Two years later he gave to the Master and Wardens of the Merchant Taylors' Company the 'Pope's Head' tavern and a shop or room belonging to it, situated in the parish of St Mary Woolnoth, Lombard Street and the parish of St Michael Cornhill, from the rental income of which the Company was to pay annual sums to twenty poor aged Freemen of the Merchant Taylors' and four Freemen of the Clothworkers' Companies, £20 annually to the school master of Burnsall Grammar School and £10 per year to the Churchwardens, of which 40s was to be used for repairs to the church and £8 to be used for repairing the schoolhouse, the bridges in the parish and the highways between Appletreewick and Burnsall. The Merchant Taylors were also to provide fuel for the poor of the parishes of St Antholin and St Andrew Undershaft.

Craven contributed to the restoration of St Antholin in 1615, but he had already moved to a house in Leadenhall Street in the parish of St Andrew Undershaft and had been elected Alderman of Lime Street Ward in 1611. There in October 1617 the King committed Lady Elizabeth Coke to Craven's custody for one month during her bitter dispute with her husband Sir Edward Coke.

Craven's partner William Parker had given £1000 towards the rebuilding of Aldersgate shortly before his death, and Craven's last public act was to lay its foundation stone on May 26 1618. Craven himself died on July 18 and was buried in St Andrew Undershaft near Parker, his 'well-beloved Friend'. On August 15 John Chamberlain wrote to Sir Dudley Carleton that it had been 'a great funeral, where there were above 500 mourners'. Craven had directed that 'for the avoiding of Tumults, which be usually occasioned at Burials, I will that nothing be given to idle Persons in the Street, on the Day of my Funeral'; nevertheless he did bequeathe money for distribution that day among the poor of various parishes, as well as sums to provide dinners for the Governors of Christ's Hospital, the Merchant Taylors' Company, the parishioners of St Antholin's and for his friends and neighbours at his house in Leadenhall Street. (He also left money not only to his family, friends and servants but also to prisoners in Newgate and Ludgate gaols and the two Compters and in the Fleet, King's Bench and Marshalsea prisons, to the poor children in Christ's Hospital, and sums 'towards the Relief and Curing of sick, sore and diseased Persons' in St Bartholomew's Hospital and St Thomas's Hospital and to Bridewell Hospital 'towards the setting of sturdy Beggars, idle and vagrant Persons on work'; the total sum bequeathed was more than £40,000). Craven left a wife (Elizabeth, daughter of Alderman William Whitmore) and five children, the youngest only about eighteen months old. His heir was his eldest surviving son (then aged ten), also called William, who inherited a fortune on his father's death. He grew up to become one of the most distinguished soldiers of his day and first Earl of Craven, marrying the sister of Charles I after she returned to England on the death of her first husband, the King of Bohemia. Thus, said Dr Whitaker (not entirely accurately) in his *History and Antiquities of the Deanery of Craven* (1808) was 'the son of a Wharfedale peasant matched with the sister of Charles I: a remarkable instance of that Providence which 'raiseth the poor out of the dust, and setteth him among princes, even the princes of his people' '.

Craven's portrait – which remained in the family until 1984 – has been attributed to Marcus Gheeraerts the Younger, an artist from Bruges in the Catholic southern Netherlands who had been brought to England at the age of seven by his artist father, a Protestant and one of many fleeing religious persecution at this time. Gheeraerts was an extremely fashionable portrait painter among patrons in the Court circle until a further wave of immigrant artists such as Daniel Mytens took his place.

Attributed to **Michiel van Mierevelt** 1567-1641 or **Daniel Mytens** 1590-1647

Sir Clement Edmondes

oil on panel
Purchased, 1951

Clement Edmondes was a scholar, soldier and diplomat, described by Anthony à Wood in *Athenae Oxonienses* (1815) as 'a learned person [...] generally skilled in all arts and sciences, and as famous as well for military, as for politic affairs, and therefore esteemed by all as an ornament to his degree and profession.' He was born – apparently of lowly parentage – in 1567 in Shrawardine, a village near Shrewsbury, Shropshire, but his family may have had connections in Essex since the Josias R Young (presumably a relative) whose name appears in the record of Clement's baptism also appears at the baptism in Essex in 1570 of a Thomas Edmonds, perhaps a brother or other near relative (Young is also recorded at the baptisms in Essex of Clement Edmondes's own sons Charles in 1603 and Henry in 1605, as well as at those of other children with the Edmondes surname in Shrawardine and Ercall Magna in the same period). In 1586 Edmondes entered All Souls' College Oxford as a clerk or chorister, graduating in 1589. He became a fellow in 1590 and three years later obtained his MA. On February 15 1597 he married Mary Clerk, an attendant to Lady Stafford, at St Alphage Church in the presence of her kinsmen Arthur B Clarke and John Johnson, a chaplain to the Queen, and of Edmondes' brother Ralph, a draper of St Martin Vintry and freeman of the Drapers' Company.

In May 1599 Edmondes was recorded as living in 'one of the parks belonging to Castle Hedingham manor', so he may have been employed at Hedingham Castle in the service of the Earl of Oxford who was the friend of many men of letters. (The Earl's tutor at Cambridge had been Bartholomew Clerke – conceivably a relative of Edmondes' wife.) By 1600 Edmondes was in the service of the Earl's cousin Sir Francis Vere, a professional soldier, to whom he dedicated his first book, *Observations upon the first five books of Caesar's Commentaries* . Vere had been appointed Governor of Brill (de Briel) in 1598 and promoted to General of the Queen's forces and of the English mercenary troops fighting in the Netherlands on behalf of the States General in the war against Spain. In July 1600 he won a famous victory at the Battle of Nieuport, and a letter from John Chamberlain to Dudley Carleton relates: 'I send news, though perhaps stale, of the great fight on Sunday week near Nieuport. One Edmunds (the translator of Caesar's Commentaries) has brought letters from Sir Francis Vere to the Council, but his relation is so partial, that it would appear that

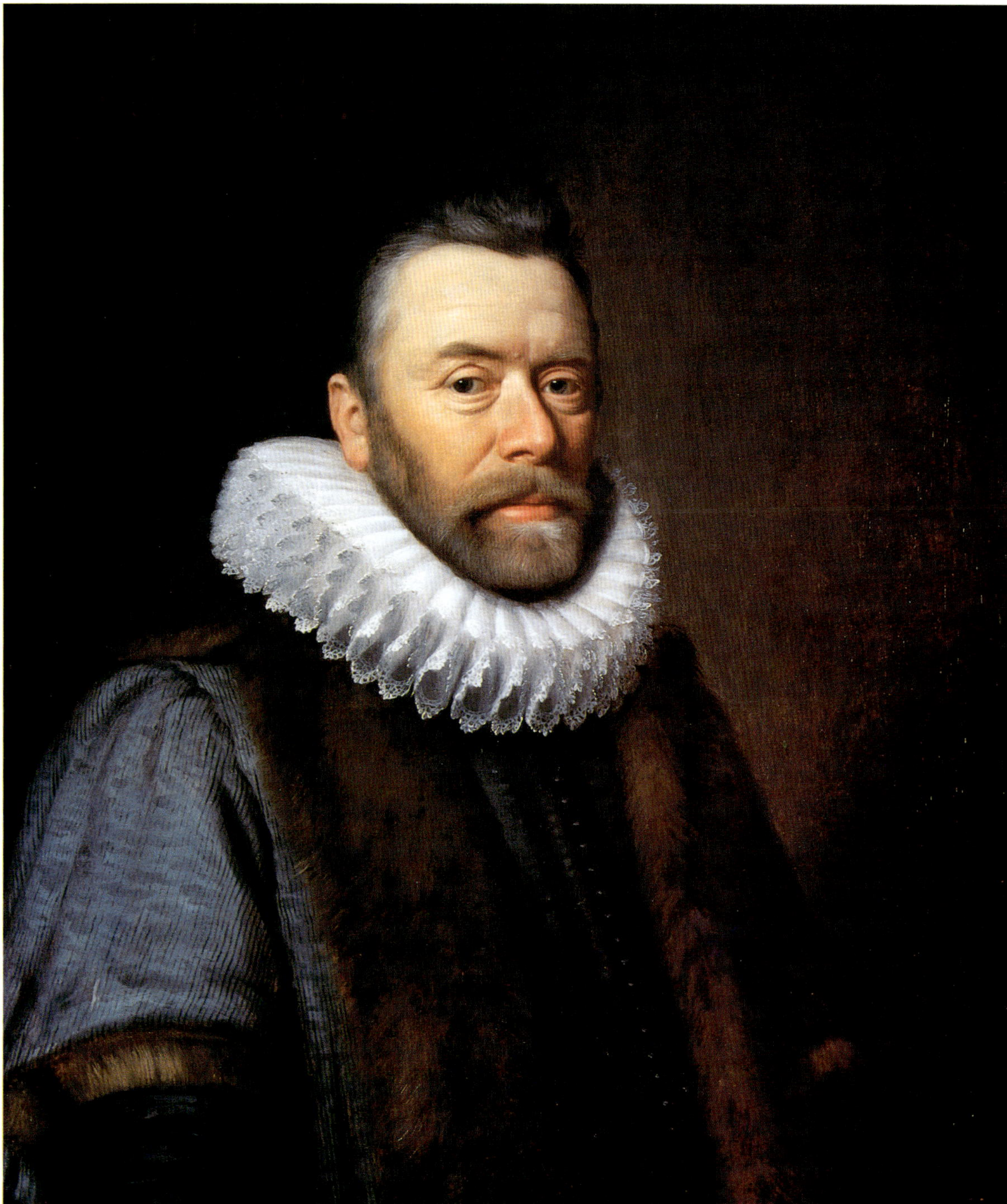

none struck but the English, and among them hardly any but Sir F Vere.' (As the memorial tablet to Edmondes in the church where he was buried described him as 'in the art militarie, by Caesar's Confessions, an understanding soldier', perhaps he had direct experience of military action while in Vere's service.)

In 1601 the Corporation of London appointed Edmondes 'colleague and assistant' to its Remembrancer, Dr Giles Fletcher, 'so that one of them do continually attend as cause shall require upon the Lord Mayor at his house when he shall be sent for and at every of the Courts of the Lord Mayor and Aldermen to do such service for this City as they shall be commanded'. On Dr Fletcher's retirement in 1605 Edmondes was promoted to his position for an annual salary of £100. His duties required him to be in close and constant communication with the Privy Council to King James I, and in 1609 he was appointed Clerk to the Council and resigned his post as Remembrancer.

In 1611 Edmondes was granted lands and estates in Berkshire seized from the recusant Sir Edward Mansfield. Two years later he was granted the office of Muster-Master General for life and at the very end of 1614 or the beginning of 1615 he was sent on a diplomatic mission to the Netherlands concerning a dispute over free trade between the merchants of the Greenland fisheries and the East India Company. On his return in 1617 Edmondes was knighted at Enfield by James I. In 1620-21 he was Member of Parliament for the University of Oxford and was appointed Secretary of State. He died in October 1622 at his house in St Martin-in-the-Fields before he could take up office and was buried in the church of St Peter and St Paul at Preston, Northamptonshire, where he had purchased the manor.

Since Edmondes was in his early forties when he resigned from the Corporation's service, this portrait – which seems to depict a slightly older man and does not include the Remembrancer's insignia of office – was probably painted somewhat later. When Guildhall Art Gallery bought it in 1951 from the dealer Spink it was attributed to Michiel van Mierevelt (although an earlier attribution to his pupil Daniel Mytens was supported by Oliver Millar, then Assistant Surveyor of the Queen's Pictures): Edmondes' portrait seems stylistically very close to the self portrait by Mierevelt dated 1626 in the Staatliche Kunsthalle, especially in the manner of painting details such as the folds of the eyelid. The most successful and well known portrait painter in the Netherlands of his day, in 1628 Mierevelt was to paint Sir Dudley Carleton, who became Ambassador to the Hague in 1616 while Edmondes was also in Holland and from the first was an important link between Dutch artists and the English court; the following year he painted Francis Vere's younger brother, the distinguished soldier Horace Vere. His pupil Mytens came to London in 1618 and was the most popular portrait painter in the court circle until the arrival of Van Dyck in 1632.

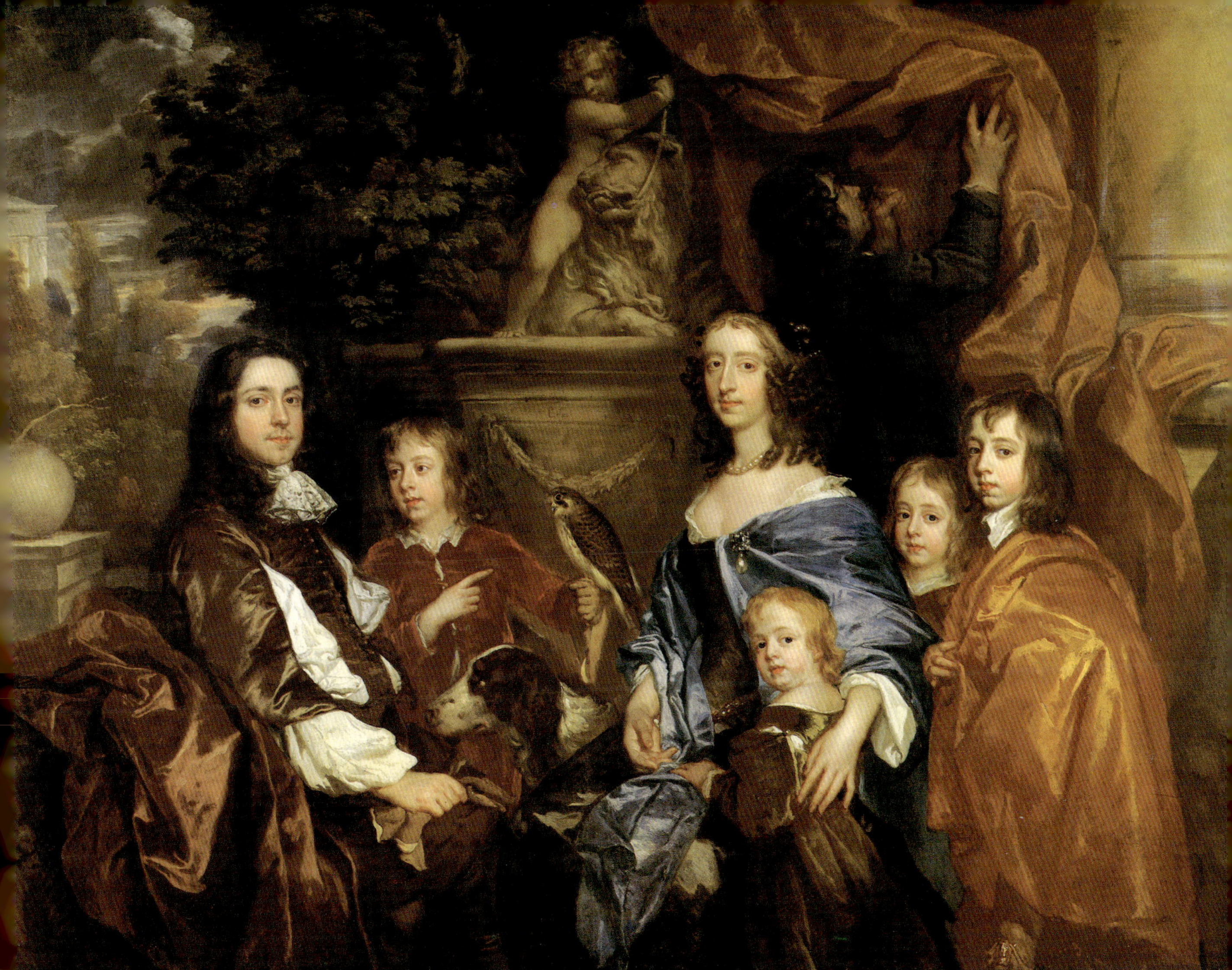

Sir Peter Lely 1618–1680

Sir Edward Hales and his family c.1656

oil on canvas

Presented by Lady Wakefield, 1944

The young man seated at the left is Sir Edward Hales (1626-1660) of Woodchurch in Kent, a zealous Royalist who in 1647 sank his own and his wife Anne Wotton's fortunes in raising forces to free the King from his imprisonment in Carisbrooke Castle at the same time as the Scots planned to invade from the north. After the Scots were destroyed by Cromwell at Preston and the Kent uprising was put down by Fairfax, Hales fled to Holland – escaping the fate of those who were hanged for their part in the plot. He remained abroad with the exiled court and died in Paris shortly after Charles II was restored to the throne.

His eldest son (also Edward, 1645-1695), probably the boy standing on the right of this picture, was the only one of his parents' four sons to survive childhood, succeeding to his father's title under Charles II. Inclined towards Roman Catholicism since his days at Oxford, he openly declared himself a Catholic in 1685 when James II succeeded to the throne. Hales was appointed a Lord of the Admiralty, deputy warden of the cinque ports and Lieutentant Of Dover Castle and, in June 1687, Lieutenant of the Tower of London. He was dismissed the following year, and when the King fled to France in December following the invasion of the Protestant William of Orange, Hales accompanied him – the King disguised as his servant. They were captured at Faversham, where Hales was detained while the King was returned to London. He was then taken first to Maidstone gaol and thence to the Tower where he was imprisoned for a year and a half. Released in October 1690 he joined the Jacobite court in exile at St Germains, and in 1692 the King rewarded him for his loyalty by making him Earl of Tenterden. Viscount Tunstall and Baron Hales of Emley. Hales applied for a licence to return to England in 1694 but died the following year without receiving it and was buried at St Sulpice in Paris.

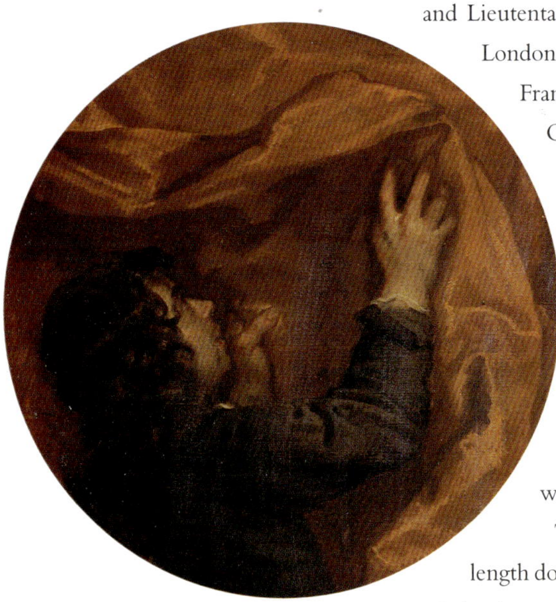

The format of this picture derives from Van Dyck's three-quarter length double portraits. Lely routinely included in his own double portraits dramatic landscape backgrounds, statues and heavy curtains, but here they may perform some symbolic function; the artist has depicted himself pushing back the curtain, apparently to reveal the statue of a putto subduing a lion. Because of Sir Edward's youthful appearance it was formerly suggested that the picture was painted before his flight to Holland and the children added later. However, not only have none of the figures been superimposed over earlier paint but all the faces were evidently painted before any of the draperies or background. They are highly finished but the hands and much of the drapery are comparatively summary and perhaps incomplete, with the reddish ground visible in many places: these elements were probably the work of a drapery painter or other assistant, whose use by portrait painters was common from the time of Mytens onwards. The picture may have been painted around 1656 when Lely travelled to Holland and is thought to have been in contact with the exiled court of Charles II.

JOHN MICHAEL WRIGHT 1617–1694

Sir John Robinson c.1662

oil on canvas

Purchased, 1970

John Robinson was born in 1615, the third son of the Venerable William Robinson DD, a cleric who eventually became Archdeacon of Nottingham and whose half brother was William Laud, Archbishop of Canterbury. (Laud was imprisoned in the Tower of London in 1640, found guilty in December 1644 of 'endeavouring [...] to overthrow the Protestant religion and to act as an enemy to Parliament', and was beheaded a month later.) His father's family had been clothiers while a great uncle had been Lord Mayor of London in 1591, and when John was fifteen he was apprenticed in London to a clothworker. He was made free by servitude of the Clothworkers' Company in 1645 and was elected to the livery of the Company later that year.

This was the beginning of a distinguished City career and great wealth. Robinson became Alderman for Dowgate Ward in 1655, Master of the Clothworkers' Company in 1656, Sheriff of London and Middlesex in 1657, Alderman for the ward of Cripplegate in 1658 and for Tower in 1663. He represented the City of London in the Convention Parliament of 1660 which recalled Charles II and Rye in the Cavalier Parliament of 1661, holding his seat until 1679. Between 1659 and 1680 he was Colonel of the Green Regiment of the London Militia and Vice-President of the Royal Artillery Company 1660-61, President between 1661 and 1680. For two periods between 1651 and 1656 he was on the Court of Assistants of the Levant Company and between 1666 and 1677 he was on the Committee of the East India Company, as well as of the Hudson's Bay Company (of which he was Governor between 1670-73).

In May 1660 Commissioners were sent to Charles II at Breda to invite him to take to the throne and Robinson was nominated one of the City's representatives. When the King landed in England on May 26 he knighted Robinson at Canterbury as he travelled from Dover to London. On 22 June the King created him a Baronet and three days later appointed him Lieutenant of the Tower of London, where he acted as godfather to Robinson's second son on August 4. The restored King took a close interest in the City's government, and needing to ensure its loyalty to the Crown he was said personally to have requested Robinson to accept election as Lord Mayor in 1662.

Holding the offices of Lord Mayor and Lieutenant of the Tower concurrently, in this portrait Robinson indicates the Collar of SS lying on a table covered with a richly coloured

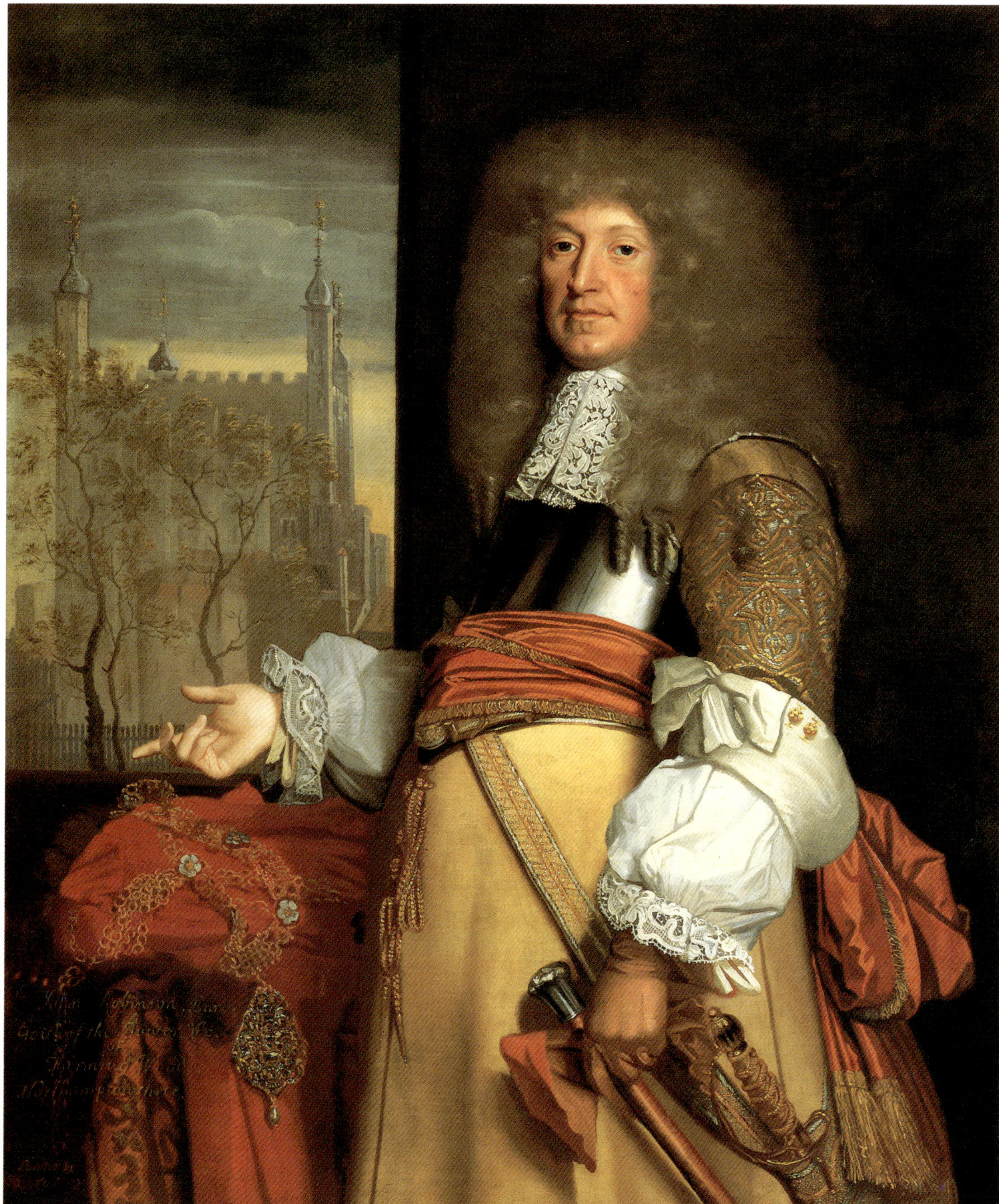

Turkey carpet, with the White Tower seen through the window behind him. Wearing a full-bottomed periwig, beneath his military breast plate Robinson also wears a buff coat with embroidered sleeves and bows, a crimson sash and lace cuffs, and carries a small sword with a gold hilt and a silver-knobbed stick. His appearance and manner tally with the description given of him by Samuel Pepys – who seems to have known him well – as 'a vain, prating, boasting man'. After spending an afternoon drinking with Robinson on March 17 1663 Pepys recorded in his diary: 'But my Lord Mayor I find to be a talking, bragging Bufflehead, a fellow that would be thought to have led all the City in the great business of bringing in the King [...] – when in every discourse I observe him to be as very a coxcomb as I could have thought had been in the City. [...] But to see how he doth rant and pretend to sway all the City in the Court of Aldermen, and says plainly that they do nor can do nor will he suffer them to do anything but what he pleases; nor is there any officer of the City but of his putting in, nor any man that could have kept the City for the King thus well and long but him – and if the country can be preserved, he will undertake that the City shall not dare to stir again – when I am confident there is no man almost in the City cares a turd for him, nor hath he brains to outwit any ordinary tradesman.' In 1666 Robinson was accused of receiving contributions towards plague relief and not distributing them; but a few years later a report to the King on 'the Character of the Lord Mayor of London and the whole Court of Aldermen' described him as 'most industrious in the civill goverrnment of the cittie, watchful to prevent anything that might reflect any prejudice or dishonour upon the King's government [...] to the great contentment of the people'.

This portrait was purchased in 1970 from one of Robinson's descendants, and another version is at the Tower of London. The Guildhall collection also holds a portrait of one of Robinson's predecessors, the ardent Puritan Sir Isaac Penington, who was Lord Mayor in 1642 and became Governor of the Tower of London in the same year. In this capacity he conducted Sir John Robinson's uncle Archbishop Laud to the scaffold in 1645 but in 1660 Penington was himself committed to the Tower, dying there six months after Robinson became Lieutenant.

Unidentified artist

Sir Charles Peers and his Daughter c.1715

oil on canvas

Presented by C J Peers, 1963

As a young man Charles Peers (1661-1737) acted as British Consul in Malaga, where with his partner William Morley he traded in salt, of which as much as two thirds of England's consumption was imported from Spain, Portugal and France. Peers returned to England in 1689 and in 1691 he was elected to the livery of the Worshipful Company of Salters, rising to become one of the City's prominent merchant elite: the Salters were one of the twelve Great Companies, their members' wealth resting on the fact that salt was a commodity required by everyone and essential for the preservation of fish and meat.

Peers was a director of the Bank of England from 1705 to 1712 except for a break that coincided with his election as Sheriff in 1707 and as Alderman for Tower Ward in 1708. In 1712 he became a Governor of the East India Company and in 1714 its Chairman, becoming Treasurer of the Honourable Artillery Company in the same year. In 1716 Peers was elected Master of the Salters' Company, and between 1720 and 1730 he was Vice-President of the HAC, becoming its President in the latter year. In 1715 he was elected Lord Mayor.

In this portrait he wears his Collar of SS and indicates the insignia of the mayoralty, the Pearl Sword which dates from the sixteenth century and the Great Mace (this one dated from 1660 and remained in use until 1735, when it was deemed past repair and a new one was made). Between them is the fur Cap of Maintenance, which is worn by the Swordbearer but doffed on civic occasions and placed on the table with the sword and mace. Standing beside her father is Mary, the elder of his two daughters by his second wife. Mary was christened January 1 1711 so was probably about five or six when the picture was painted. In her stiff dress and holding a small whip, she echoes Sir Charles's severity in her own oblique and impassive gaze, the only clue to her childish shyness and uncertainty her tentative clasp of her father's unresponsive fingers.

It has been suggested on stylistic grounds that this portrait may be by Charles Jervas (c.1675-1739). Peers could have met Jervas through the influential Whig politician Sir Robert Walpole, who became Chancellor of the Exchequer and First Lord of the Treasury in the year of Peers's mayoralty; Peers would have met him through his involvement with the Bank of England and the East India Company. The Irish-born Jervas painted Walpole's portrait around 1708-10, and it is known that Walpole's influence obtained him further commissions.

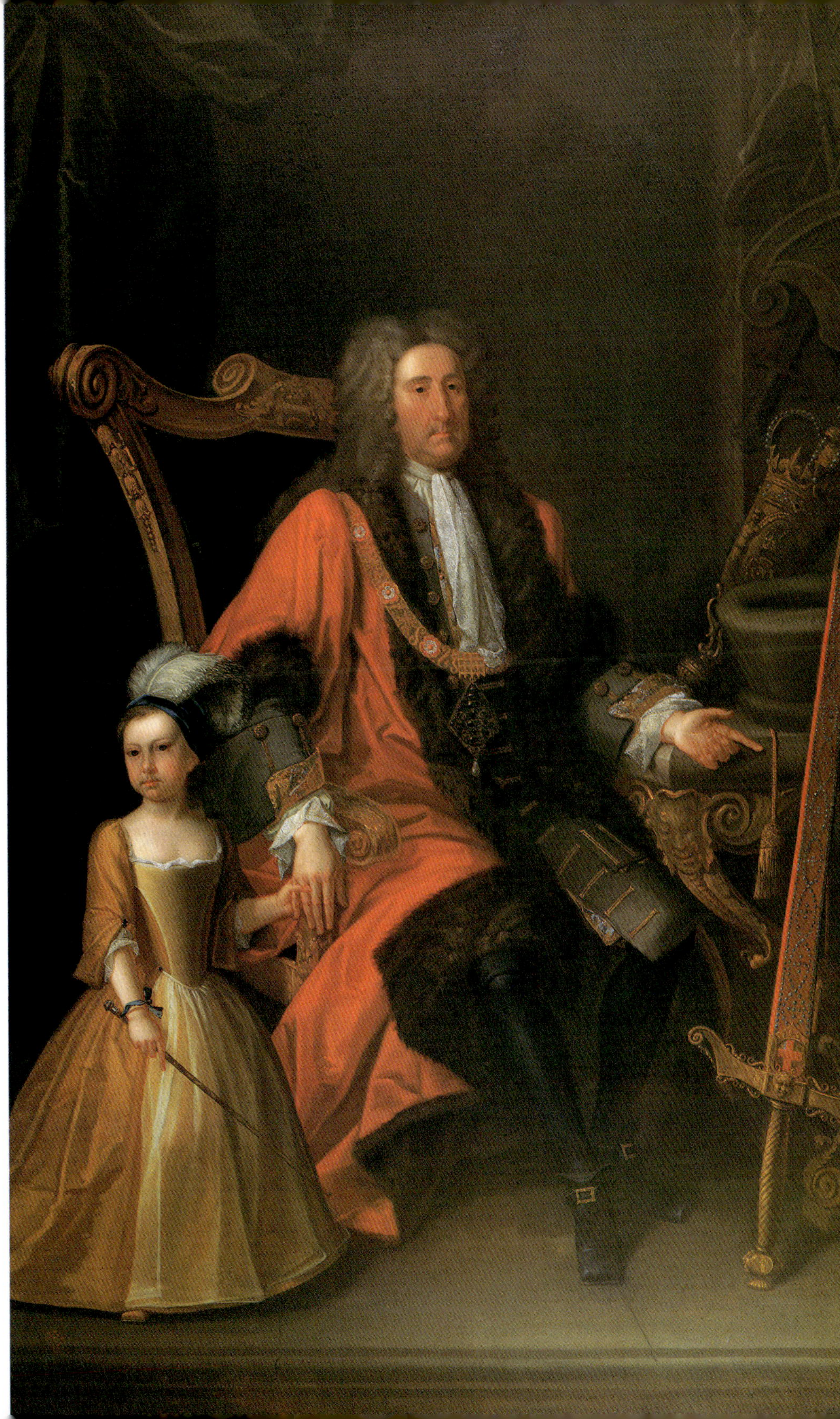

Nathaniel Dance 1735-1811

Sir Robert Kite, Lord Mayor 1766

oil on canvas

Presented by Major General Sir James Kidney Cockburn, 1843

Sir Robert Kite was born in about 1708, the son of Benjamin Kite, a feltmaker in the parish of St Thomas Southwark. At the age of fourteen he was apprenticed to Robert Browne, a skinner, and gained his freedom of the Skinners' Company in 1730. Kite went on to amass considerable wealth and status, with a residential and business address (from 1752) at 40 Cannon Street and a country seat at Lubenham Court, Leicestershire.

Kite was elected Member of the Court of Common Council for Candlewick Ward in 1747 and continued to represent it until 1756, the year in which he became both Master of the Skinners' Company and Alderman of Lime Street Ward. He was elected Sheriff on August 8 1760 with a majority of 105 over his rival, and on October 16 he was knighted with his co-sheriff William Hart by George II at Kensington. When Kite was elected Lord Mayor of London in 1766 the Skinners' Company had their barge repainted and gilded for his procession to Westminster on Monday November 10, provided the barge master with a new silk gown and his mate with a new scarf, together with jackets and caps for the men and gowns and caps for fifty-eight pensioners of the Company, thirty gold chains for gentlemen and cockades, ribbons and bells for participants in the procession. After Kite had taken his oath before the Barons of Exchequer at Westminster Hall, the procession returned to Guildhall for a grand entertainment attended by many of the nobility and persons of distinction, followed by a ball.

Kite's year as Lord Mayor was marked by very severe winter weather on the heels of a failed harvest: there were food riots in the countryside and many rioters were hanged. On Friday January 2 1767, reported the *Gentleman's Magazine*, 'the tide rose so high in the river Thames that the damage done by it is estimated at 50000*l*', while on the following Monday 'the navigation of the river Thames was stopt at Fulham Bridge by the severity of the weather', and the next day 'the snow was so deep throughout the whole kingdom, that the like has not been remembered by the oldest man living; many people have perished; cattle and horses have been buried and dug out; the stage waggons have been delay'd; the post boys have been bewildered and some frozen to death; in short the severity of the season is universally felt, and the distresses of the poor in many places are inexpressible.' To alleviate their suffering, the government placed a temporary ban on exports of grain, flour and meal and on the distilling of liquor from grain; meat and dairy products were imported from

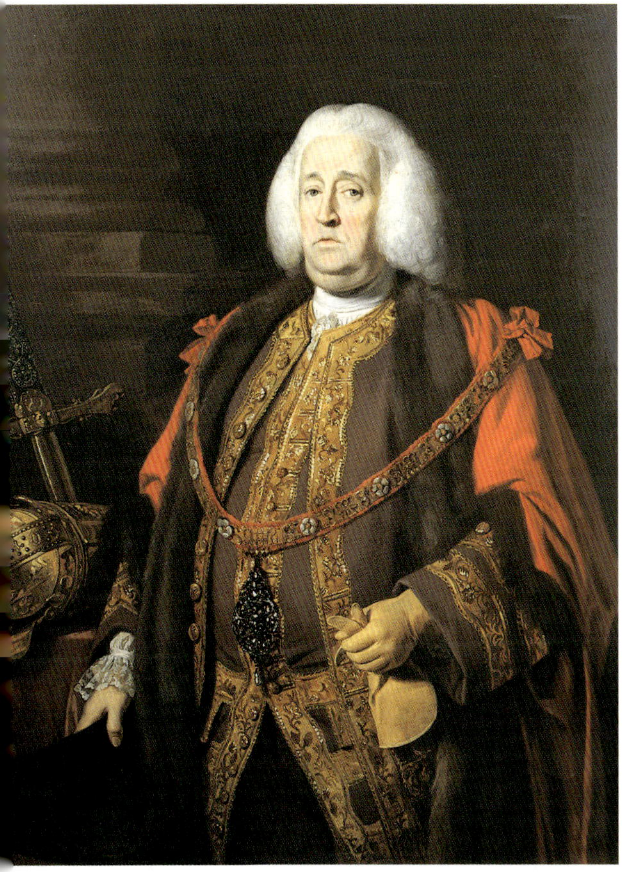

Ireland, and the duty was lifted from grain imported from the American colonies. Despite these measures, on January 13 1767 the Court of Alderman learnt that most of the flour destined for the London market was on board barges and other vessels prevented from reaching the City by the frozen river, while supplies were in any case reduced by the 'riots and tumults in those counties from which London was principally supplied'. A week later the Court of Common Council ordered £1,000 to be drawn from the Chamber of London to aid those among the poor who were not already getting parish relief, and opened a private subscription to which Kite donated £100 from his own purse. Shortly afterwards the Committee which he headed as Lord Mayor distributed £1,315 to the needy. (Nevertheless, on Lord Mayor's Day the following year, reported the *Gentleman's Magazine*, 'some unthinking persons treated the late Lord Mayor with great indignity, under a false notion that his Lordship was the occasion of raising the price of bread; tho' nothing could be more false.')

Kite may have met Nathaniel Dance through his father, the architect George Dance who was the Corporation's Surveyor and Clerk of Works until his death in 1768. The artist painted this portrait not long after his return to England from a twelve years' stay in Rome, where the elegance and glamour of Pompeo Batoni's portraits had been the most significant influence on his style. Like Batoni's, Dance's clientele in Italy had consisted of young Englishmen making the Grand Tour, and the connections he made there helped to establish him as a successful portrait painter on his return. Here Dance's debt to Batoni is equalled by his striking grasp of his subject's character and manner.

After Kite's death in September 1772 this portrait passed to his great-niece Christian Kidney. On her own death in 1826 she left it to Major-General Sir James Cockburn of Langton provided he took the surname Kidney in addition to his own, intending that it should pass after Sir James's death to a Mr George Hart 'if living'. In a later codicil to her will, 'seeing the ill state of health of Mr George Hart', she bequeathed the portrait to the newly established National Gallery 'to [be] by the Nation kept as a memorial of a truly honest Gentleman and the work of a fine painter'. Presumably Cockburn was unaware of this codicil when he presented the portrait to the Corporation of London seventeen years later.

Thomas Hardy 1757-c.1805

Brass Crosby, Alderman of Bread Street Ward 1787

oil on canvas

Presented by the Hon Irish Society, 1892

Brass Crosby (1725-1793) was born in Stockton-on-Tees and apprenticed to an attorney in Sunderland before coming to London and practising first in Little Minories and then moving in 1752 to Seething Lane. He was elected Member of the Court of Common Council for Tower Ward in 1758, and having accumulated a substantial fortune through his successive marriages to two wealthy widows, in 1760 he purchased the office of City

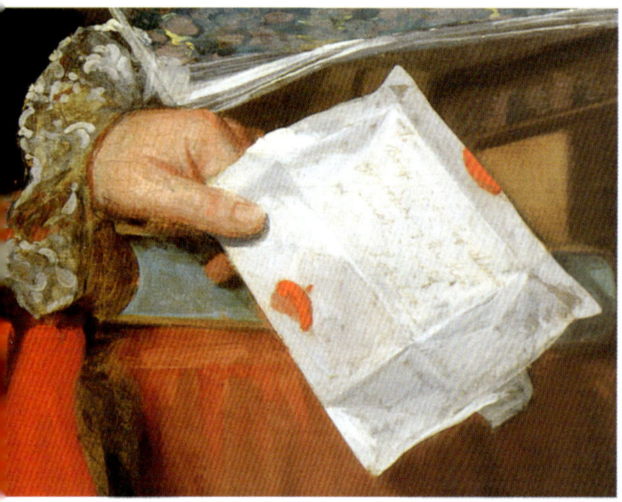

Remembrancer for £3,600 (and sold it again the following year). In 1764 he was elected Sheriff and in 1765 Alderman of Bread Street Ward. Crosby was originally a member of the Musicians' Company but in 1766 he translated to the Goldsmiths, becoming Prime Warden the following year (it was necessary to belong to one of the twelve Great Companies in order to be Lord Mayor). In 1768 he was elected Member of Parliament for Honiton, representing it until 1774 (in which year he unsuccessfully contested the City of London, and again in 1784). Elected Lord Mayor in 1770, a few months later Crosby was involved in a famous dispute with the House of Commons – see page 32. Crosby was President of the London Workhouse and President of the Honourable Artillery Company from 1780 to his death in 1793, Treasurer of Bethlem and Bridewell Hospitals in 1781-82 and their President from 1782 to 1793; in 1785 he became Governor of the Irish Society. On his death, the *Gentleman's Magazine* noted: 'his activity as a magistrate, and his strict attendance on that variety of public stations which he fulfilled are almost proverbial. Possessed of an uncommon degree of patience, integrity and sagacious penetration, few men have ever been better qualified to preside at a public meeting; and his eminent abilities and independent spirit will long be remembered. [...] He was buried, with great funeral pomp, [...] at Chelsfield church; the funeral being attended by all the Aldermen who have passed the chair, the common-council of Bread Street, and his neighbour Peter Perchard Esq. The body lay in state at Chatham-place, and the procession, consisting of 10 coaches and six, and the empty carriages of several of the mourners, was preceded by the two city marshals, and by the city sword-bearer, carrying the black sword of state, used only on solemn occasions like the present.'

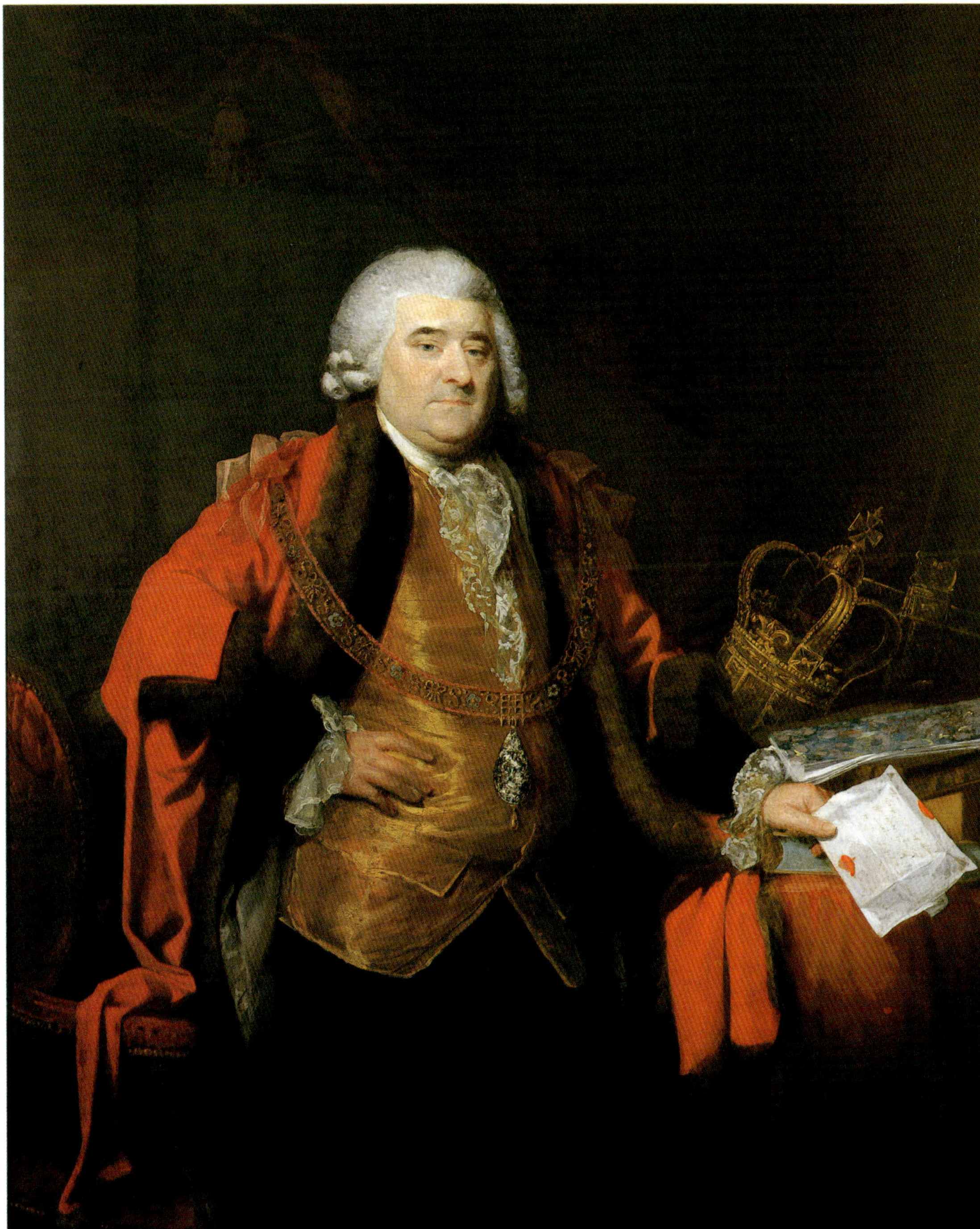

Robert Edge Pine c.1730-1788

Alderman Oliver 1771

oil on canvas
Purchased, 1990

The Whig politician Richard Oliver, a member of the Society of the Bill of Rights, became a freeman of the Drapers' Company in June 1770. A month later he was elected Alderman of Billingsgate Ward in place of the famous Whig William Beckford and was called to the Livery of the Drapers' Company and admitted to its Court of Assistants. In the same month he was also elected in Beckford's place as MP for the City, and in August he was elected Master of the Drapers' Company.

Oliver was a supporter of the radical politician John Wilkes, but following his involvement with Brass Crosby in the celebrated case of the Printers versus the House of Commons – when Crosby and Oliver were imprisoned in the Tower and, as the *Gentleman's Magazine* reported, Wilkes 'completely baffled every attempt to implicate him in the censure' – Oliver refused to serve as Sheriff with his former friend, telling Wilkes that his political views and intentions were very different from his own; he did however serve as Sheriff in 1772-73. Neither Wilkes nor Oliver would hardly be considered democrats today in that they were both members of the slave owning classes, Wilkes on his estates in Jamaica and Oliver on his in Antigua, to which he retired in 1778: he died in 1784 on the last leg of a voyage home to England from the island of St Kitts.

When Brass Crosby was elected Lord Mayor on September 24 1770 he placed his hand on his heart and told his fellow citizens 'that at the risk of his life he would protect them in their just privileges and liberties'. A few months later Crosby and Oliver became involved in a dispute with the House of Commons which was popularly perceived as one over press freedom. In reality it was about maintaining the City's right to control its own affairs, and coincided with its opposition to a bill then passing through Parliament for the embanking of Durham Yard in order to build the Adelphi. On Feb 8 1771 a Member of the House of Commons, Colonel Onslow, complained to the House of a breach of privilege by R Thompson, the printer of the *Gazeteer* and John Wheble of the *Middlesex Journal* in printing parliamentary debates. They were ordered to attend at the House, and when they failed to appear on March 12 a royal proclamation for apprehending them was issued and a reward offered of £50 each. The next day the printers of six more newspapers were ordered to attend the Commons. On March 15 John Wheble was apprehended by an Edward Twine Carpenter (perhaps a friend acting collusively) and brought before

CAP.
XXIX.

Alderman Wilkes at Guildhall. Finding that Carpenter had no complaint to make against Wheble but only the authority of the Proclamation, and furthermore had – it was claimed – used force against him, he discharged the printer (but also gave Carpenter a certificate to enable him to claim the £50 reward as directed by the Proclamation).

The next day John Miller, printer of the *London Evening Post*, was also taken into custody at his home by William Whitham, a messenger from the House of Commons acting on a warrant from the Speaker. A constable was sent for and Miller accused Whitham – who had grabbed his arm – of assault. They were taken to the Mansion House and brought before Crosby, Wilkes and Oliver. The Lord Mayor asked Whitham if he had applied to a City magistrate to back the warrant he held from the House or to any Peace Officer of the City to assist him, and the reply being no Crosby then said that 'so long as he was in that high office, he looked upon himself as a Guardian of the Liberties of his Fellow-Citizens; that no power had a right to seize a Citizen of London, without an authority from him or some other Magistrate; and that he was of opinion, the seizing of Miller and the warrant were both illegal.' He then discharged Miller but committed Whitham for assault. Half an hour later the printer of the *Gazeteer*, R Thompson, was apprehended at his home in Newgate Street and brought before Alderman Oliver: Oliver set Thompson free and gave his captor a certificate to enable him to claim his reward.

On the morning of Tuesday March 19 the House of Commons ordered Crosby as Member for Honiton to attend in his place to explain his conduct. A hand bill was dispersed round the City rousing support for him: 'To the Liverymen, Freemen, and Citizens of London. Although our Lord Mayor has been confined to his room for sixteen days with a severe fit of the gout, and is still much indisposed, he is determined to be this day in his seat at the House of Commons, to support your Rights and Privileges, even though he should be obliged to be carried in a litter. He leaves the Mansion House at one of the clock.' The *Gentleman's Magazine* reported that looking feeble and infirm but in good spirits, Crosby had left accompanied by his Chaplain and by Alderman Oliver and that 'a prodigious crowd of the better sort were at the Mansion house and in the streets near it, who testified their approbation by repeated huzzas, which were continued quite from the Mansion house to the House of Commons. On his arrival there, one universal shout was heard for near three minutes, and the people, during the whole passage to the House, called out to the Lord Mayor as the *People's Friend, the Guardian of the City's Rights, and the Nation's Liberties*.'

Crosby defended his actions to the Commons by arguing that 'he had only done his duty as Chief Magistrate of the City of London, having acted conformable to his Oath and the Charters of the said City, by which he was bound to protect the Persons, Property and Franchises of his Fellow-Citizens.' He was then allowed to withdraw on account of his illness, and handbills having been again distributed around the City urging Freemen and 'the Citizens of London, and all Friends of Freedom in this Metropolis' to turn up at the House of Commons and conduct the Lord Mayor back 'in Triumph' to the Mansion House, he returned home about five o'clock attended by crowds of people who unharnessed the horses from Crosby's coach at St Paul's and pulled it back to the House themselves.

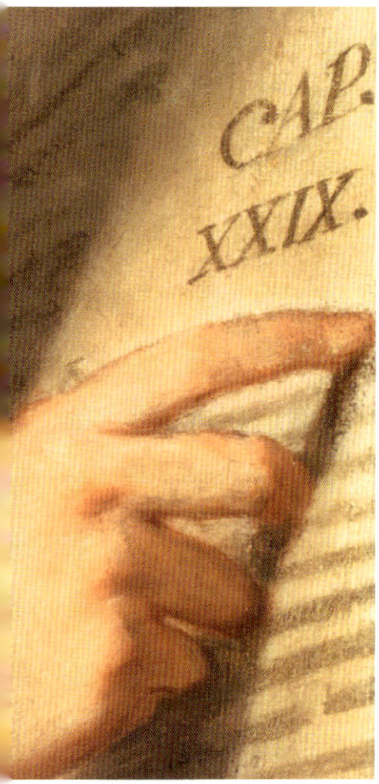

As Members of the House of Commons, Crosby and Oliver could not refuse their summons to appear without being in contempt but when John Wilkes refused an order to attend on March 20 they could not compel him, for although he had been elected for Middlesex in 1768 the House had already expelled him. When they again demanded his attendance together with Crosby and Oliver on Monday the 25th, the Court of Common Council unanimously resolved 'That the thanks of this Court be given to the Right Hon. the Lord Mayor, and the Aldermen Wilkes and Oliver, for having, on a late important occasion, supported the Privileges and Franchises of the City, and defended our excellent Constitution,' and appointed a Committee of four Aldermen and eight Commoners to assist them in their defence, empowering them to employ such Counsel as they thought appropriate and to draw on the Chamber of London for any sum not exceeding £500.

At two o'clock on the 25th the Lord Mayor and Alderman Oliver went from the Mansion House to the House of Commons, crowds of supporters lining the streets along the route. The House debated whether to censure or expel Crosby or to commit him to the Tower, but by half-past ten 'his Lordship finding his strength exhausted, and being unable to bear the pain and fatigue any longer, begged permission to retire; which being granted, he returned to the City, attended as before by a vast concourse of people, who took the horses from the coach, and drew it all the way to the Mansion house, testifying their approbation of his Lordship's conduct by the loudest acclamations and repeated shouts of applause.' At about 3 am Alderman Oliver was committed to the Tower of London. (He was allowed to go home to sleep at his own house in Fenchurch Street, and the Serjeant at Arms collected him between 7 and 8 am to take him to prison in a coach.) There he was visited by many members of the nobility and members of the House of Commons, and the Common Council agreed that 'the expence of Mr Alderman Oliver's table, during the time he remains prisoner in the Tower, be defrayed by the City.' Next day the Lord Mayor returned to the House of Commons, attended by such crowds that, as the *Gentleman's Magazine* reported, 'the Justices and High and Deputy Constables of Westminster were all attending, and the Guards, both horse and foot, were ordered to be in readiness, in case any tumult should arise.' The House resolved that in freeing Miller and discharging the messenger Crosby was in breach of the privilege of the House and it would have committed him to the custody of the Serjeant at Arms, but on 'his Lordship's observing, that if any offences had been committed, he was the greatest offender, and that he longed to join his brother in office' Crosby was himself committed to the Tower. He arrived there about 4 am on Thursday March 28 after some hours' sleep at the Mansion House 'and was lodged at Mrs Bradshaw's, on the parade, next door to the Bloody Tower. His Lordship, notwithstanding his indisposition, was in great spirits.' Imprisoned without trial, in April Crosby and Oliver were twice brought up before the Court of Common Pleas on a writ of Habeas Corpus but were remanded back to the Tower. During his imprisonment Crosby was presented with the Freedom of the City of Worcester and of the town of Bedford, and addresses from Camarthen, Pembroke and Cardigan and Newcastle, Stratford and Honiton, and he was visited in the Tower by the principal members of the opposition as well as by many of his City friends; outside on Tower Hill the mob burnt effigies of Colonel Onslow and the Speaker. It was not until Wednesday May 8, when Parliament was prorogued, that Crosby and Oliver were freed. Summonses issued from Guildhall called on the Aldermen and the Common Council to conduct them in state to the Mansion House, and their procession was attended by the Honourable Artillery Company. Cheering crowds lined the streets and the City was illuminated, while celebrations were also held across the country. The Court of Common Council voted silver cups (now in the Mansion House) to both men commemorating their stand in support of liberty and free speech, while an obelisk was erected in Crosby's honour in the centre of St George's Circus, Blackfriars Road, not far from his home in Chatham Place, Blackfriars Bridge.

Among those who visited Crosby and Oliver in the Tower was a portrait painter with radical sympathies, Robert Edge Pine, who had already painted John Wilkes around 1764. The whereabouts of the portrait Pine now painted of Crosby in the Tower are now unknown, but the portrait illustrated on page 33 is the one he painted of Oliver, indicating the Biblical passage which is perhaps in chapter twenty-nine of *Jeremiah* (eg verse seven, 'And seek the peace of the city whither I have caused you to be carried away captive, and pray unto the Lord for it; for in the peace thereof shall ye have peace'); however the actual chapter is far longer than the one illustrated here.

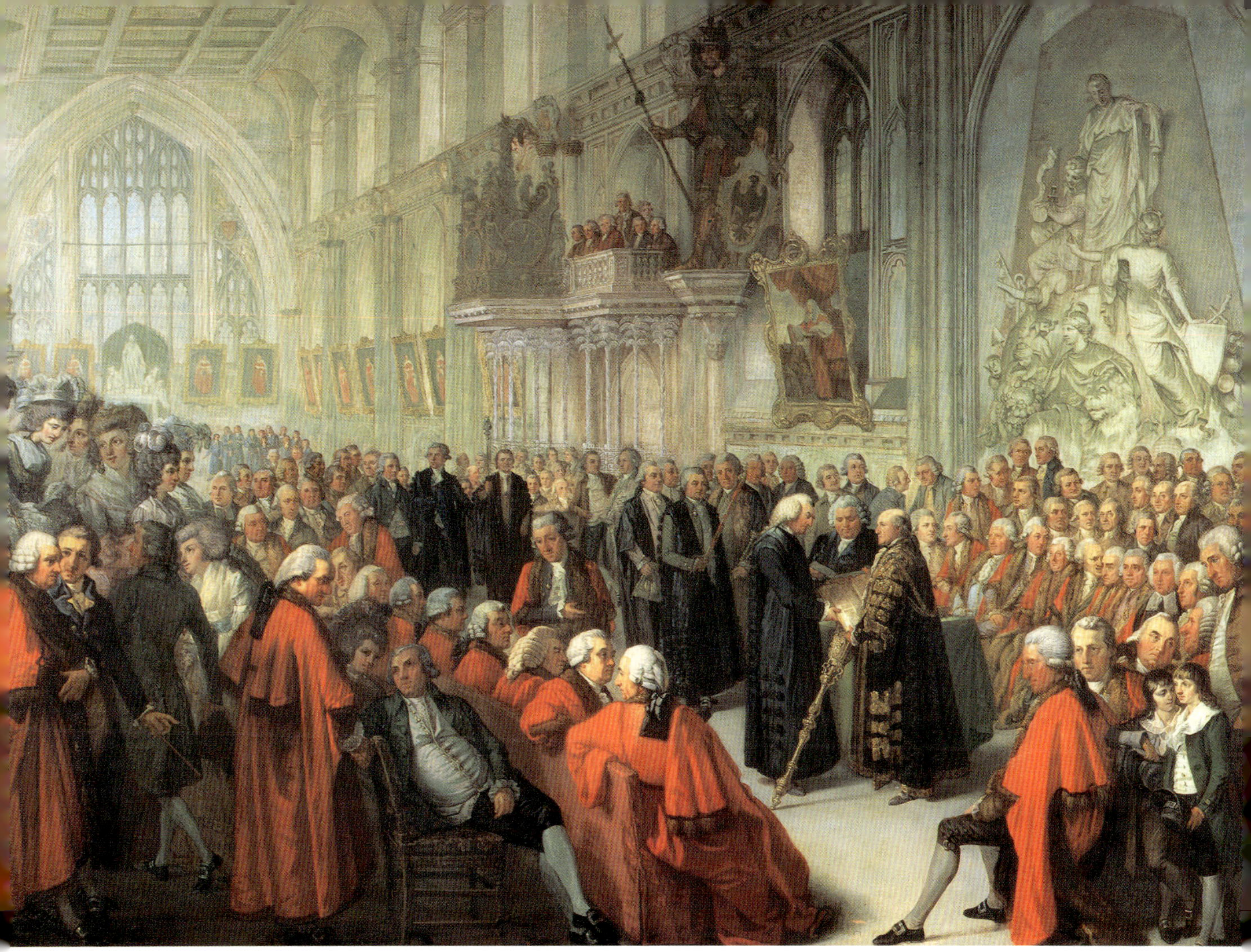

WILLIAM MILLER c.1740-1810

The Ceremony of Swearing In Alderman Nathaniel Newnham, November 8 1782

oil on canvas

Presented by Alderman John Boydell, 1793

Nathaniel Newnham was a sugar-baker who went on to found the private bank of Newnham, Drummond, Tibbitts and Tanner. A liveryman of the Mercers' Company, he was Master in 1786. He was elected Alderman of Vintry Ward in 1774 and Sheriff in 1775, and in 1780 he was elected Member of Parliament for the City, continuing to sit until 1784. He was Lieutenant Colonel of the Honourable Artillery Company from 1781 to

1784, Colonel of the Orange Regiment from 1783-1789, the Fifth London Militia between 1789 and 1794 and the West London Militia from 1796 to1809; and between 1794 and 1796 he was Lieutenant Colonel of the East London Militia. Newnham was also President of St Thomas's Hospital from 1782 to his death in 1809 and from 1804 he was a Collector of Orphan's Coal Duties.

Newnham became Lord Mayor in 1782, and here he is seen seen in his black and gold state robe being admitted in Guildhall on November 8 in the Silent Ceremony, described in 1787 in *Kearsley's London Register*: 'The Order for Simon and Jude's Day. The old Mayor shall have so many of the Aldermen as Dine with him, come to his place at Eight of the Clock in the Morning, in their Violet Gowns furred, with their Violet Cloaks furred, and Horses, and the Sheriffs to fetch him to the Hall, and there tarry in the Council-Chamber, with the Company of either of the Lords before them: and after they have been together a certain space, come forth into the Orphans' Court, and put on their furred Cloaks, and go to the Hustings Court [at the east end of Guildhall, seen here]: and there being set in order, the Common Crier maketh Proclamation, commanding every Man to keep silence.

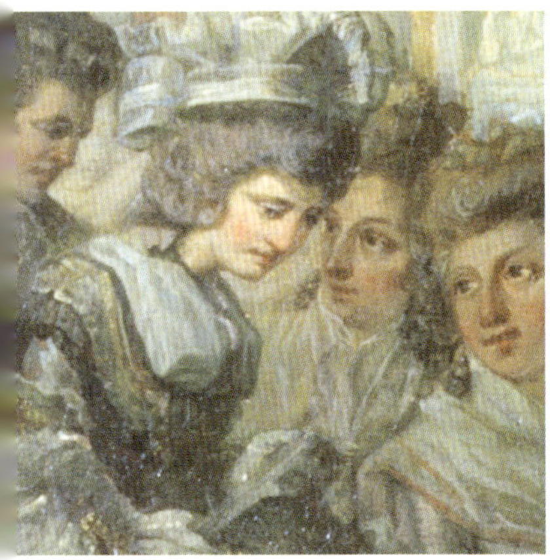

Then Mr Town-Clerk giveth him his Oath; and when he hath taken his Oath, the old Lord ariseth and giveth the new Lord his Place, the old Lord taking the new Lord's Place; and then Mr Chamberlain delivereth first to him the Sceptre, next the keys of the Common Seal, lastly, the Seal of the Office of the Mayoralty: after Mr Sword-Bearer giveth him the Sword. Then they arise and putteth off their Cloaks, and the old Lord rideth Home with the new Lord to his Place, and there leaveth him, and as many of the Aldermen as dine with him. And the old Lord, with the rest of the Aldermen, ride to his Place, the Sword born [sic] before him; and so after Dinner the Aldermen depart Home at their Pleasure.'

Newnham is seen standing facing William Bishop, the Common Cryer, who holds the book from which he reads his Oath with the Town Clerk, William Rix, between them; behind stands Heron Powney the Sword Bearer with the upraised Sword of State. Beside the Swordbearer is William Montague, the Clerk of the Chamber of London, apparently standing in for the Chamberlain, John Wilkes, who sits among the spectators at the right and turns to whisper in his neighbour's ear. An unidentified man named as 'Mead' in the printed key to the painting holds the City Purse containing the mayoralty seal. Among the Aldermen (here in their scarlet gowns) and other dignitaries present is Brass Crosby, seated next but one to Wilkes. The two small boys at the bottom right are nephews of the Lord Mayor, while the new Lady Mayoress is seen leaning forward in a group of ladies on the left. Directly below is John Boydell, elected Alderman the previous August. His nephews John and Josiah Boydell stand on either side, while Josiah's wife Jane and Boydell's niece Mary are among the group of Ladies accompanying the Lady Mayoress; Mary lived with the Alderman, who had no children of his own and looked upon her as a daughter.

It is difficult to make an appealing and lively picture from ceremonial subjects like this with many different individuals who all need to be recognisably portrayed. Miller solves the problem by giving his composition a receding diagonal axis that enables him to successfully incorporate all the figures. Although the group of the Lord Mayor, Town Clerk and Common Cryer form a still, silent focal point, in order to animate his composition and provide a recognisable view of all the other figures Miller sacrifices the dignified silence that in reality must have attended the ceremony and composes the figures into chatting groups enlivened by the dramatic use of light and shadow.

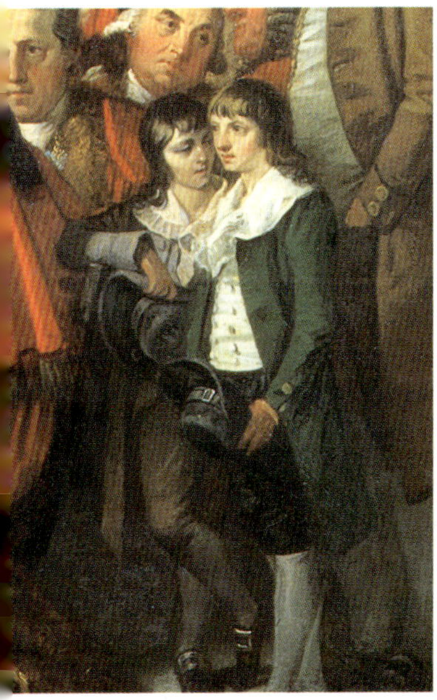

The painting offers an interesting record of the appearance of the Guildhall at this time. Prominently depicted in the right background is the monument to William Pitt, Earl of Chatham, which had been commissioned from John Bacon in 1779 and was not completed until 1783. At the far (West) end of the Guildhall is J F Moore's monument of 1770 to William Beckford (it is now located on the South wall and a doorway occupies its site in this picture). The giant figure of Magog – one of a pair with Gog made in 1708 by Captain Richard Saunders to replace earlier wicker figures destroyed in the Great Fire of 1666 – is seen against the North Wall (both figures were destroyed in the air raid of 29 December 1940 and were replaced with the present versions in 1958). Beside this figure is a gallery filled with dignitaries and a balcony bearing a clock, both supported on slender painted iron columns in the form – incongruously – of palm trees. The coffered wooden ceiling replaced one which had been destroyed in the Great Fire and was itself replaced in 1865 by a wooden hammer-beam one, which in turn was burnt in the air raid of December 1940 and replaced with the current version by Sir Giles Scott. Next to the Chatham monument is Sir Joshua Reynolds's portrait of Lord Chief Justice Sir Charles Pratt (later Lord Camden), commissioned by the Corporation in 1764. The other pictures shown are some of the twenty-two portraits by John Michael Wright of the 'Fire Judges' commissioned by the Court of Aldermen between 1670 and 1675. Together with some Royal portraits which also hung in the Hall they had been restored and rehung only a couple of years before Nathaniel Newnham's election as Lord Mayor. They were badly damaged when the Guildhall was burnt on the night of December 29 1940 and being considered difficult or even impossible to restore in 1952 all but two were deaccessioned.

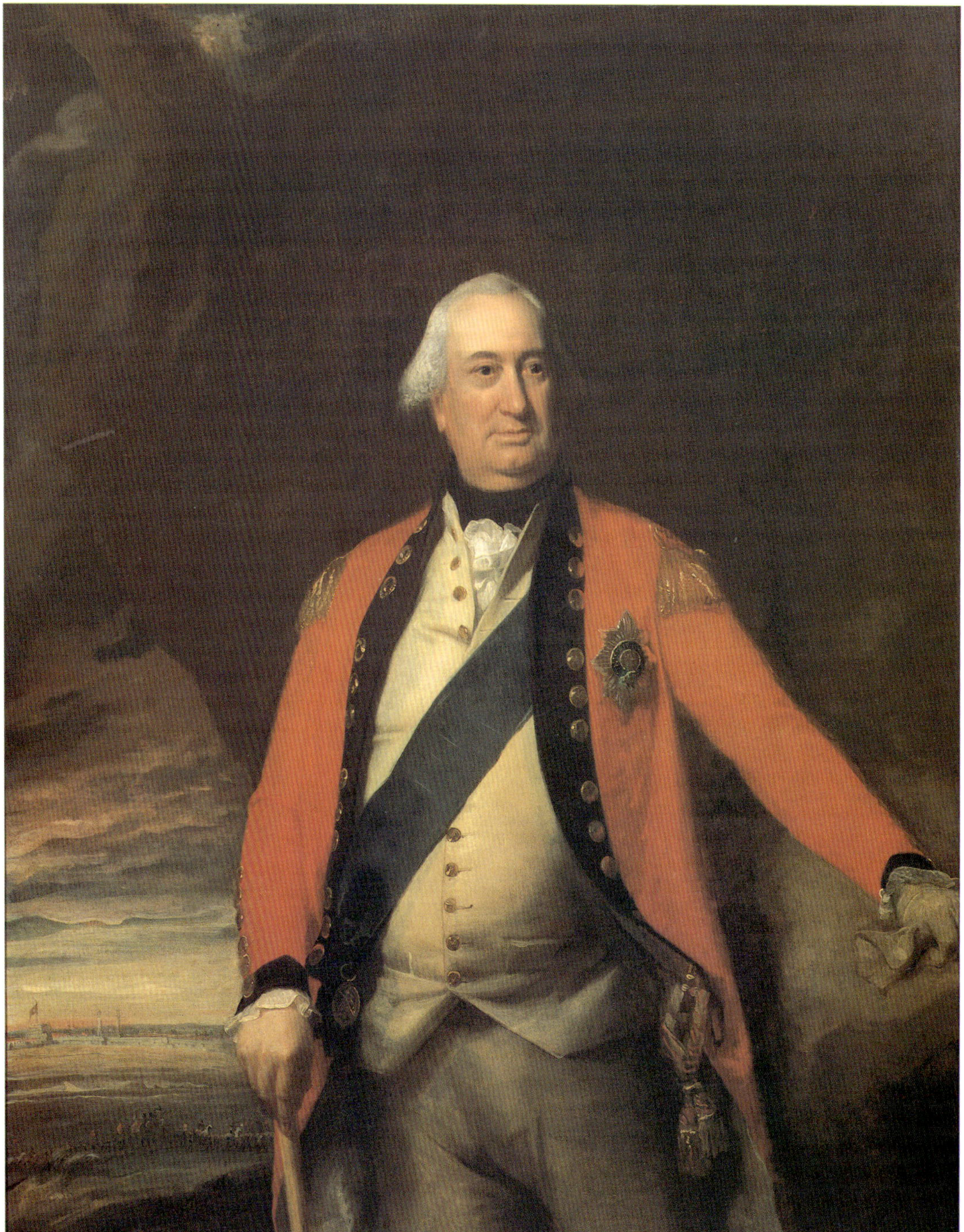

JOHN SINGLETON COPLEY 1738-1815

Marquis Cornwallis 1795

oil on canvas

Presented by Alderman Boydell, 1795

As the background indicates, Charles, second Earl Cornwallis (1738-1805) – a professional soldier who served with distinction in the American War of Independence – is portrayed as Governor General of India, the post to which he was appointed by the Prime Minister William Pitt in 1786 with the task of reforming its civil and military services. Cornwallis was created Marquis in August 1792 in recognition of his conduct in the third Mysore war against Tippoo Sultan, and on October 4 the Court of Common Council resolved unanimously to thank him, Major-General Meadows and the officers and soldiers under Cornwallis's command in India, 'for their gallant conduct and essential service rendered their country' and to present Cornwallis with the Freedom of the City in a gold box of one hundred guineas' value 'as a testimony of the high esteem of the Citizens of London'. It was not until 3 February 1794 that Cornwallis arrived in England, and on April 5 a deputation of Members of the Court visited him to request that he accompany them back into the City to receive the Freedom, the Lord Mayor addressing him in these words:

'Your Lordship will do the Citizens of London the justice to believe that they were not among the last to feel and to acknowledge the high and important service you had rendered to your country. The rank which our City holds in the commercial world, and the great share which she enjoys of the trade with India, naturally led her numerous inhabitants to attend with anxious eye the progress of those very interesting scenes your Lordship was engaged in, and which by you have been brought to so glorious a conclusion. It was therefore with the utmost joy, and with the most perfect unanimity, that the Common Council of this City expressed by their Resolution the high sense they entertained of your great merits.

'And here, my Lord, if superior consideration did not restrain me, how easy and how pleasing it would be for me to dwell on so delightful a theme. For me who, in my situation of an East India Director, have had better opportunities than any of my fellow Citizens to follow your Lordship in the discharge of the several duties of your high station, and therein to contemplate the good Governor, the wise Legislator, the brave Soldier, the great General, the excellent Statesman, and the moral, good Man, how grateful to my feelings woud it be to speak of the improved state of the provinces you have governed; of the British character everywhere exalted; of confidence restored among the Native Princes; of protection effectually given by wise and beneficent Laws to the many millions under the

British Government; of great military talents displayed; and, above all, of that signal instance of wisdom and moderation – unknown and unexampled in the history of India – the stopping in the full career of victory, and foregoing the glory which would have attended the surrender of the proud Capital of Mysore, to grant peace to a vanquished foe, and thereby change a bitter enemy into a useful and respectable ally.'

This picture is one of several portraits of contemporary military or naval heroes which Alderman Boydell commissioned for the Common Council Chamber as part of his scheme to decorate the Chamber with improving subjects and to promote living artists. He had a long-standing business relationship with the American artist John Singleton Copley and had lent him two hundred guineas in 1787 to enable him to travel to Hanover to take the portraits of the mercenary allied officers which he needed for his monumental painting *The Defeat of the Floating Batteries at Gibraltar*, which the Corporation had commissioned three years earlier. In February 1794, when Copley petitioned the Court of Common Council for an additional payment, the Court agreed only on condition that he repay the Alderman, and as he refused they paid Boydell themselves in March 1795 and withheld the balance of the agreed addition until Copley was forced to swallow his pride and claim it four years later. It is a measure of Boydell's well-known decency that he commissioned Copley to paint this portrait soon after Cornwallis's arrival in England and at the height of the dispute over his payment. He paid the artist £67.14s.6d. for the picture on 5 June 1795 and it was already hanging in the Common Council Chamber by 18 June when he formally asked the Corporation to accept it.

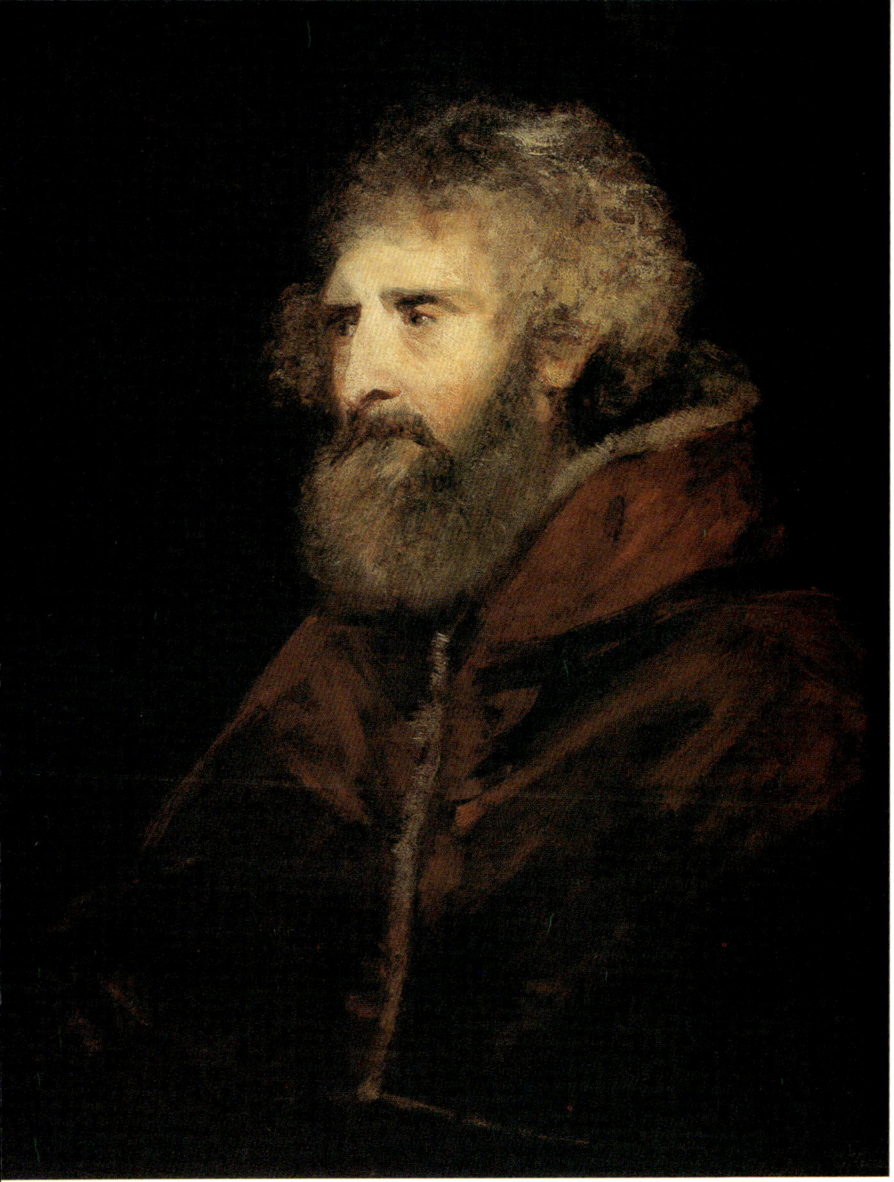

Sir Joshua Reynolds

1723-1792

Pope Paviarius

oil on canvas

Presented by Lady Wakefield, 1944

This picture entered the Guildhall collection with the title 'The Banished Lord', which it had held at least since 1850, but in 1985 Dr. Martin Postle identified the correct title and the sitter as one of Reynolds's best-known models, George White the pavior – painted in the guise of a Renaissance pope.

George White was said to tramp from York to London every spring and back to York in the autumn; when asked why he did not spend his winters in London, he was said to have replied 'Why Sir? because coals be cheap in the North and warmth be the life of an old man.' Reynolds discovered White at work in the street and exhibited his first study of him at the Royal Academy in 1771; he was also the model for the Count in *Count Ugolino and his Children in the Dungeon* (exhibited 1773) and *A Captain of Banditti*. As well as sitting for Reynolds at his Leicester Square studio White also posed for students in the Royal Academy Schools where his muscular physique made him a popular model, and for many other artists including Nathaniel Hone who painted him in 1775 as *The Conjuror* and as *St Paviarius* (now lost). White was also taken up by the anatomist Dr John Hunter, who used him as a model in lectures, but in the end his irregular lifestyle was said to have induced Hunter to part with him (although he and Reynolds provided the pavior with an allowance that rendered his last years comfortable).

Sir Joshua Reynolds 1723-1792

Thomas Tomkins, Writing Master 1789

oil on canvas

Presented by the sitter, 1790

Thomas Tomkins (1743-1816) was the finest and most famous calligrapher of his day. Together with his partner John Reddall he kept a writing school in Foster Lane, but he was also the intimate friend of Sir Joshua Reynolds and many other artists, whom he used to astonish by the ease with which he could draw a perfect circle. From 1776 Tomkins was employed by the Corporation to prepare Addresses, Honorary Freedoms and Thanks, copies of which adorned the Chamberlain's Parlour. He also produced many of the Royal Academy's addresses to the King and in 1789, the year in which he transcribed the Academy's congratulations to the King on his recovery from illness, he commissioned Reynolds, its President, to paint this portrait of himself. There is a tradition that Tomkins gave Reynolds twenty sittings for the portrait and that when it was finished the artist said 'I will now give you a specimen of my writing,' and with his brush signed and dated the back of the canvas *J. Reynolds, pinx., 1789* (the canvas has since been lined so the inscription cannot be verified). It was one of the last seven portraits Reynolds sent to the Royal Academy before having to give up painting in 1790, having lost the sight of one eye the previous year.

After a long illness Tomkins died aged seventy-four at his home in Sermon Lane, Doctors' Commons on September 5 1816, bequeathing his portrait in these words:

'I give and bequeath to Richard Clark Esq. Chamberlain of the City of London for the time being, and to all succeeding Chamberlains of this City, my Portrait painted by Sir Joshua Reynolds, P.R.A. being the last picture from the pencil of that celebrated Master, – with a request that it may be placed in the Chamberlain's Parlour with the duplicates of the Honorary Freedoms and Thanks presented by the Lord Mayor, Aldermen, and Common Council, to the distinguished Heroes, Statesmen, and other eminent Characters, who have so ably and successfully exerted themselves to secure our invaluable Constitution from the ambitious designs of our envious and powerful Enemies.'

The Chamberlain accepted the portrait on October 1 1816 with, according to the writer of a letter on October 14 to the editor of the *Gentleman's Magazine*, 'that dignified politeness, and feeling, which marked his esteem for the Testator, and his sense of the value of the bequest. A more appropriate situation for the Portrait could not have been selected, surrounded as it is by the elaborate productions of his pen which adorn that room.'

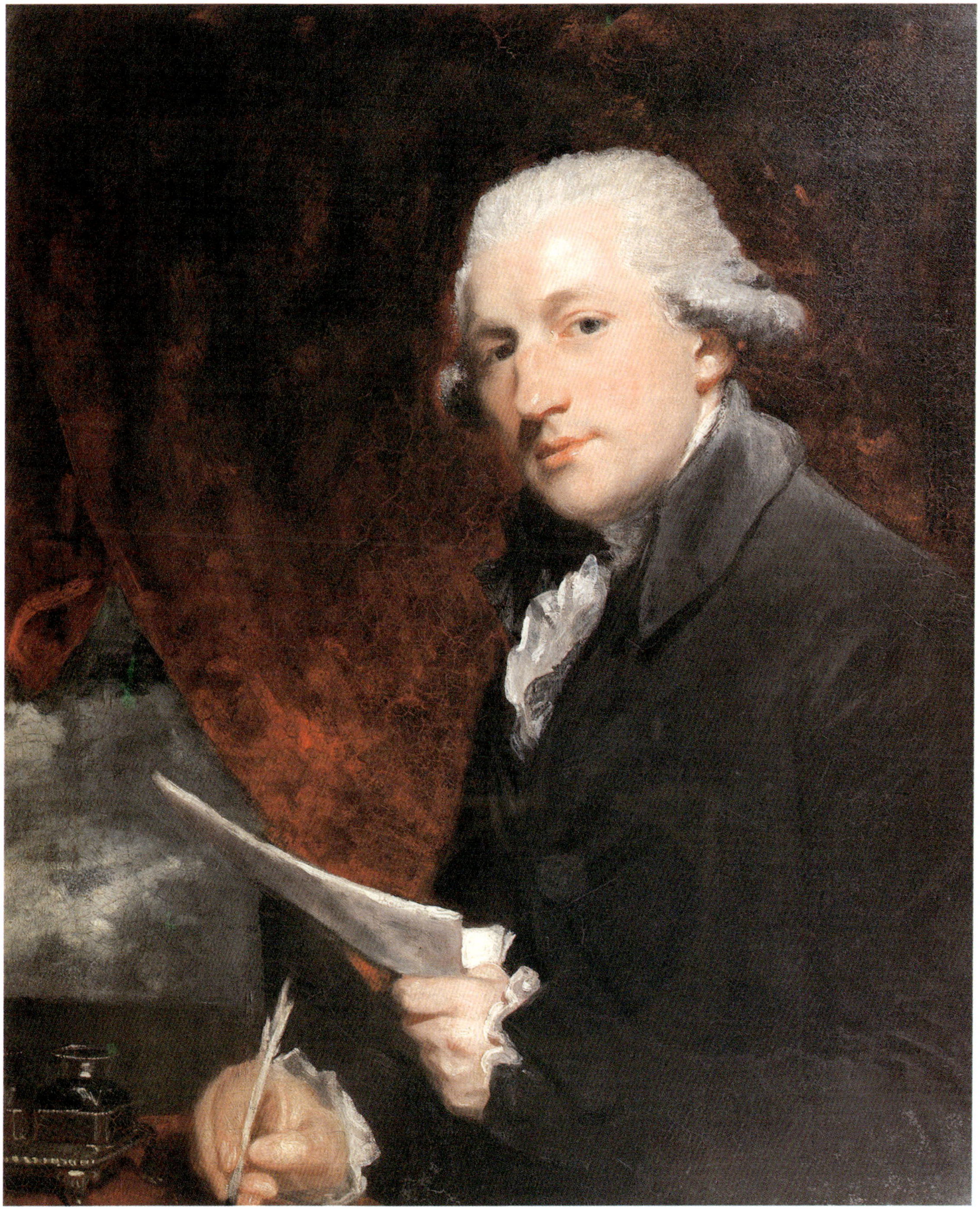

Sir Thomas Lawrence 1769-1830

John Philip Kemble as Coriolanus 1798

oil on canvas

Presented by the Earl of Yarborough, 1906

John Philip Kemble (1757-1823) was a son of Roger Kemble, a travelling actor-manager. His eleven other children included Sarah, who married William Siddons and became one of England's greatest tragic actresses, and Charles, who was also an actor and the father of the celebrated Fanny Kemble. John Philip was originally intended for the priesthood and attended a Catholic seminary and then college in France, but his passion for the theatre led him to an acting career and his first stage appearance in Wolverhampton in 1776. Between 1783 and 1802 he appeared at Drury Lane as Hamlet and in *King John, Othello* and *King Lear*, but he was particularly associated with the role of Coriolanus, which he first played in his own adaptation of Shakespeare's play at Drury Lane in January 1789 and in which he retired from the stage in June 1819.

Lawrence had known the Kemble family from boyhood and was particularly friendly with John Philip. This portrait is one of four powerful depictions of the actor in his finest roles – the others are Rolla in R B Sheridan's *Pizarro* (exhibited RA 1800), Hamlet (RA 1801) and Cato (RA 1812) in Addison's eponymous play – in which Lawrence employs striking composition and dramatic chiaroscuro to express psychological intensity. In the scene depicted here (Act IV, scene V) the banished Roman hero waits in disguise at the house of Tullus Aufidias, intending to join with him against Rome.

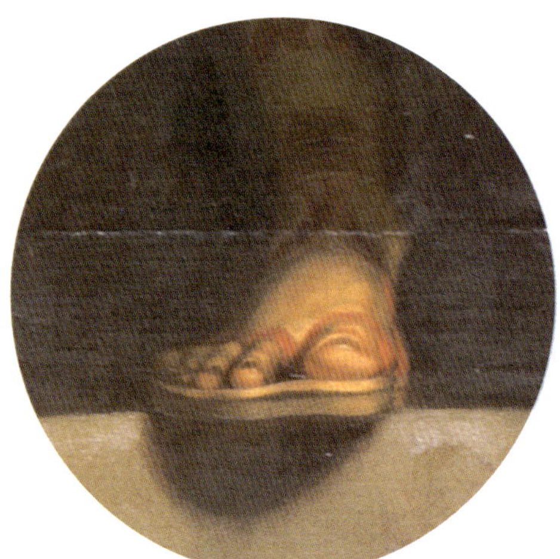

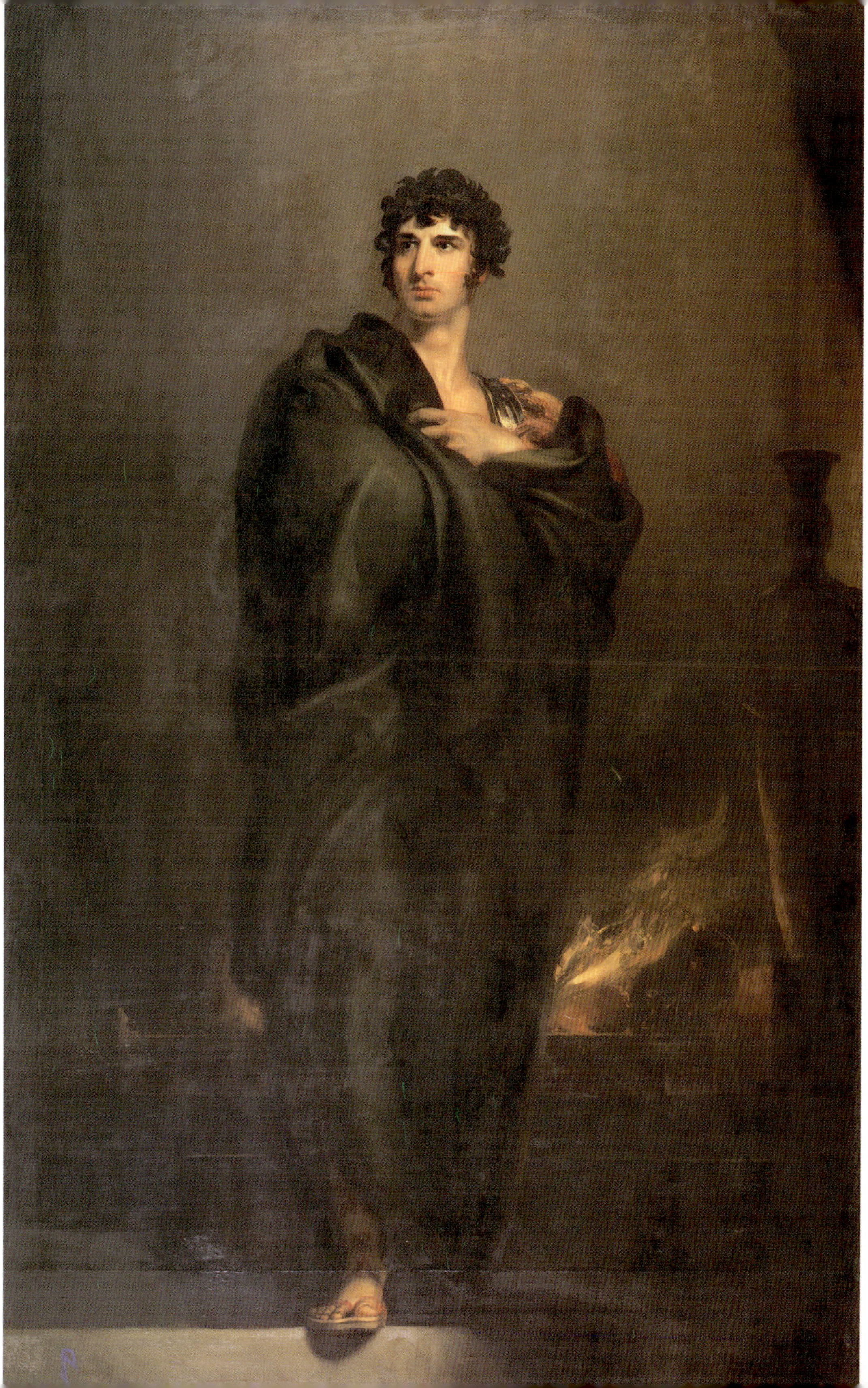

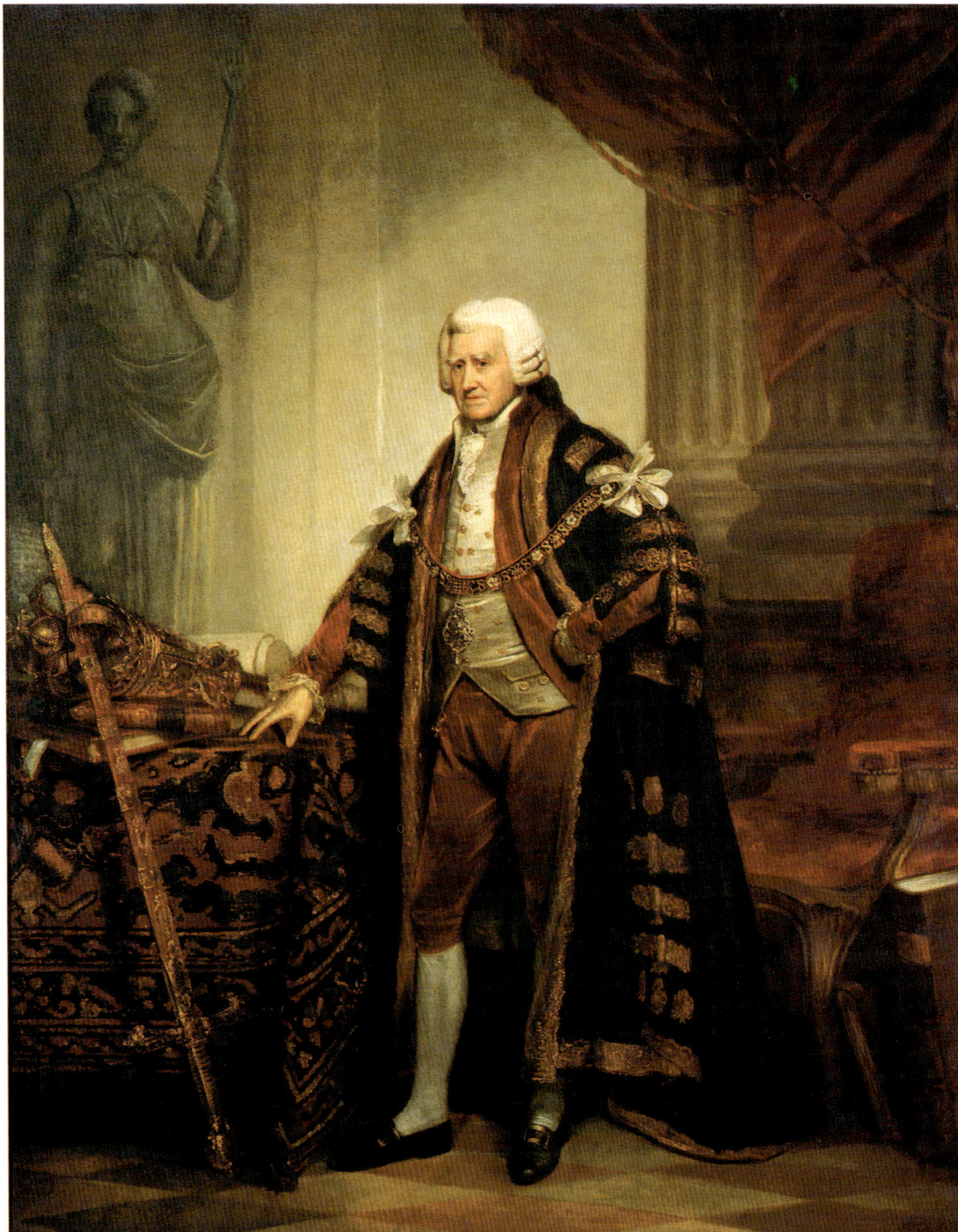

Sir William Beechey 1753-1839

Alderman John Boydell 1801

oil on canvas
Commissioned by the Corporation, 1800

John Boydell was born in 1719 in Dorrington, Shropshire and at the age of 20 came to London where he attended drawing classes at the St Martin's Lane Academy and apprenticed himself to the engraver W H Toms. He set up as an engraver, publisher and print seller in Queen Street in about 1750, soon moving his flourishing business nearby to no. 90 Cheapside. Boydell was elected Member of the Court of Common Council for the Ward of Cheap in 1758 which he represented until 1770 and again from 1772 to 1782, the year he was elected Alderman. He was Master of the Stationers' Company 1783-4, in 1785 he was Sheriff and in 1790 he became Lord Mayor.

Boydell was the first to recognise the potential in publishing engravings after paintings by other artists and he revolutionised the English print trade, exporting prints to France when hitherto the trade had been in the other direction. Boydell also hoped to establish a native school of history painting in England at a time when the public was largely indifferent to it and to promote the interests of artists whenever possible. In 1786 he commissioned thirty-three leading British artists to paint pictures of Shakespearean scenes from which he published engravings, and three years later he opened the Shakespeare Gallery in Pall Mall which exhibited thirty-four pictures (the number had increased to 162 by 1802). The artist James Northcote said that his 'friend and patron Alderman Boydell [...] did more for the advancement of the arts in England than the whole mass of nobility put together', while the King himself 'spoke in high terms of his public spirit and encouragement of the arts'.

Northcote's painting *The Death of Wat Tyler* was one of the twenty-three canvases which Boydell presented to the Corporation of London between 1792 and 1801 for the specific purpose of decorating the new Common Council Chamber, designed by George Dance in 1777. (Despite the loss of several of the largest pictures during World War II they still form the core of the Corporation's eighteenth-century holdings.) In his *Description of Several Pictures Placed in the Common Council Chamber of the City [...] for the Benefit of the Servants who shew the Pictures* (1794) Boydell explained that his motives were: 'First, to show my respect for the Corporation and my fellow-citizens. Secondly, to give pleasure to the public, and Foreigners in general. Thirdly, to be of service to the Artists, by shewing their works to the greatest advantage; and, Fourthly, for the mere purpose of pleasing myself.

The poor, and all in the inferior stations of life may profit by the advice which many of the subjects in this collection will impart to them.' Among the pictures were Miller's *Oath to Alderman Newnham* 'one of the finest Ceremonies ever exhibited in this or any other Country' (page 37); portraits of contemporary heroes like Lord Heathfield by Reynolds (returned to Boydell's nephew Josiah after 1804 and now in the National Gallery) and Copley's *Lord Cornwallis* (page 40); and naval battles by Richard Paton and Robert Dodd. Boydell also commissioned four frescoes of allegorical subjects from J F Rigaud, but the Chamber was too cold and damp for this medium and the frescoes rapidly deteriorated before being painted over in 1814.

On February 27 1800 the Court of Common Council resolved 'that the Members of this Corporation, grateful for the Delight afforded to them as often as they assemble in this Court by the Splendid Collection of Paintings presented by Mr Alderman Boydell, entertaining an affectionate sense of the honour done to them by that celebrated Patron of Arts, and proud of the Relation in which they stand to him, as Fellow-Citizens, do in Testimony of these feelings, request him to sit for his Portrait to an artist of his Choice, conscious however, that hereby they are only requesting him to confer a new gratefication on themselves, and their Successors, and unwilling that amid such and so many Remembrances of Sublime Character and illustrious Actions, his Portrait should be wanting, who, discerning in the discovery and munificent in the encouragement of Merit in others combined, in his own Character private Integrity with Public Spirit and solid Honesty with a highly cultivated Taste.' On November 19 1801 the Court ordered the Chamberlain to pay Beechey £210 for the portrait, although it was not for another two years that £89 16s was paid for its frame.

Boydell's early years were spent with his paternal grandfather, a clergyman, and the rest of his life was regulated both by religious faith and by a strong sense of honour and duty. In the background of this portrait is a statue of a female figure holding a wand which terminates in an open palm on which is an eye, while beneath her other hand is a beehive, symbol of industriousness. That these references must have been specified by Boydell himself is revealed by the notebook (c. 1793, Guildhall Library, Manuscripts) in which he made prescriptive notes on three subjects which he originally envisaged as forming part of the Common Council scheme – *Industry and Prudence, Honour and Riches*, and *Liberality and Fame* (in the event only one subject – *Conjugal Affection, or, Industry and Prudence* was commissioned from Robert Smirke). While Liberality would have been represented – as Boydell himself chose to be – as 'Lord Mayor of London in his Entertaining Robes, with the Collar of SS & the Sword and Mace', *Industry* was to be expressed, he wrote, by 'a Beautiful

Female Figure leaning upon a capstan, dressed in white Robes, encircled by green leaves. In her right hand she is holding a sceptre [...]; on top of the sceptre is placed the little figure of a hand with an eye in the palm of it: & by the side of the figure is placed the statue of Plutus, and a bee appears flying over her head. The Capstan alludes to the manual exercise & fatigue of the industrious, and the white robes encircled with green leaves denote that candour, hope and good intentions direct industrious persons in the paths of virtue, and that they attentively regard the rules of honesty. The sceptre points out the power and patronage of Princes, who graciously encourage the hand of Industry, this is particularly indicated by the hand on the top of the sceptre. The eye in the palm of the hand, signifies that by prudence, Industry should always be regulated [...]'.

In Beechey's portrait the figure of Plutus, god of riches, is omitted and the bee – which would surely have been too small to be visible – is replaced by its hive. The all-seeing eye on the palm of the open hand is also, although Boydell does not mention it, an ancient symbol of God.

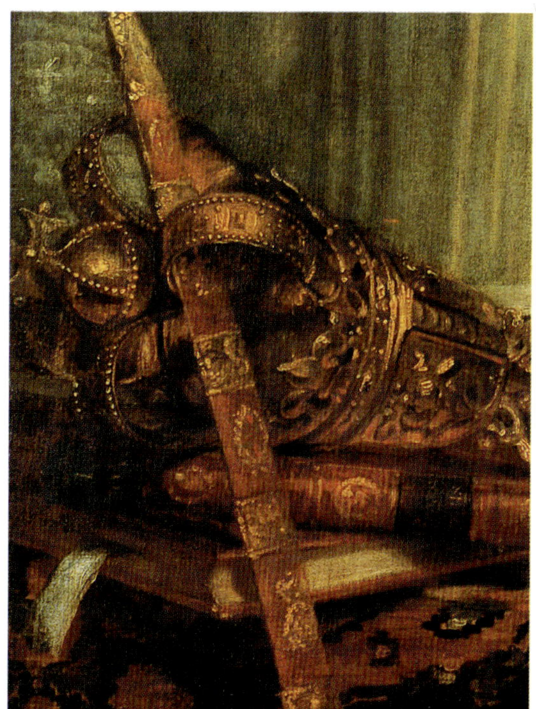

MATHER BROWN c.1761-1831

Sir John Eamer, Lord Mayor 1801

oil on canvas

Bequeathed by Mrs Claxson, 1873

Sir John Eamer (1750-1823) started out with a small grocer's shop in Leadenhall Street, but by 1800 he was an important wholesale grocer with a business and residential address in Wood Street. He was a member of the Salters' Company and became its Master in 1805. Eamer had been elected Sheriff in 1794 (the Salters possess a portrait of him as Sheriff painted by Brown around this time) and the following year he became Alderman for Langbourn Ward, which he represented until his death; he was knighted on April 15 1795 and stood unsuccessfully for Ilchister in 1796. Eamer was Lieutenant Colonel of the West London Militia between 1796 and 1803, and from 1803 to 1820 he was Colonel of the East London Militia. He became Lord Mayor in 1801 and from 1814 to his death he was Police Magistrate for the Borough of Southwark.

In 1805 Eamer had to face a court martial but was 'honourably acquitted of all the charges' and his five accusors were displaced from the regiment. When he appeared on the parade ground for the first time after his acquittal, *The Times* reported that 'his reception was highly flattering. The officers and privates of the regiment, after having presented arms to their Colonel, gave him CHEERS, to testify their veneration for their Commanding Officer, and their joy on the occasion of his triumph. They have also come to the unanimous resolution of presenting Sir John with a sword.' This portrait may have been painted to commemorate this event.

Mather Brown was born in Boston, Massachusetts but settled in England in 1781. His first sitters had American connections but in 1789 he became Portrait Painter to the Duke of York and in 1791 to the Duke of Clarence. Perhaps his best known painting is *The Sons of Tippoo Sultan delivered as Hostages to Lord Cornwallis* (1793), but both the quality of his work and his success declined after 1800. As well as the Salters' Company portrait and the Guildhall picture, Brown also painted a now untraced portrait of Eamer in the uniform of another of the volunteer militia that succeeded the original trained bands, the London and Westminster Light Horse Volunteers.

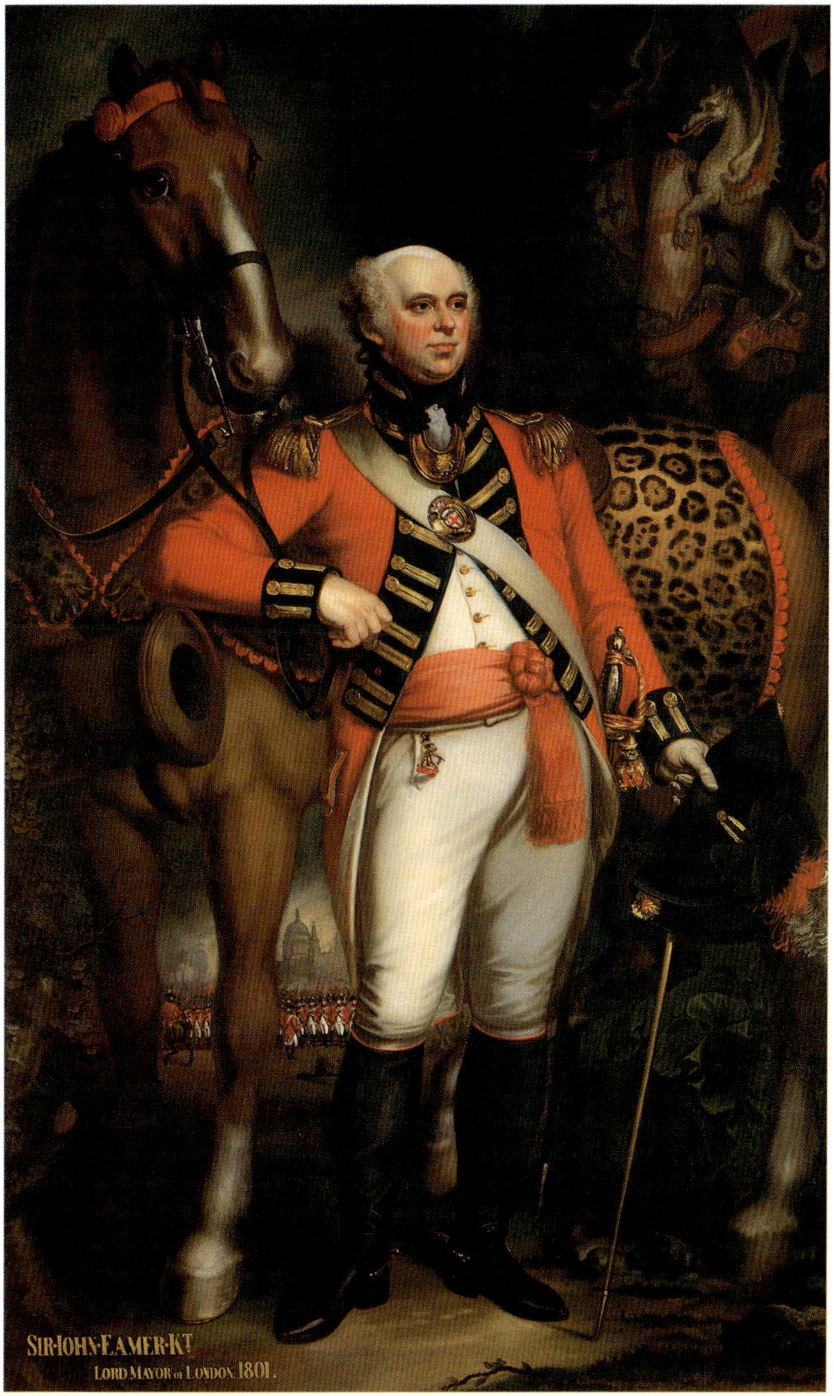
SIR·IOHN·EAMER·KT
LORD MAYOR OF LONDON. 1801.

Mary Martha Pearson 1799-1871

Samuel Birch 1837

oil on canvas

Presented by C N the sitter's granddaughter, 1877

Samuel Birch (1757-1841) was born in London, the son of a well-established pastrycook and confectioner of no. 15 Cornhill. He was educated at a private school until the age of 14, when he was apprenticed to his father. In 1781 – at the age of twenty-four – he was elected a Member of the Common Council for Cornhill Ward, becoming Deputy in 1789. On the outbreak of the French Revolution he proposed that volunteer regiments should be formed, and although at first the idea drew no support in the Common Council, when the measure was adopted in 1804 Birch was made Lieutenant-Colonel Commandant of the 1st Regiment of Loyal London Volunteers. Birch was commended by the King and was voted the Freedom of the City of Dublin in 1805 and 1806 for his advocacy of the Protestant ascendancy in Ireland; in 1807 – the year in which he became Alderman of Candlewick Ward – he is reputed to have stamped the words 'No Popery' on his buns. Birch was Sheriff in 1811 and in 1814 he was elected Lord Mayor.

Birch was a member of a debating society that met in the Kings Arms Tavern, Cornhill. He was also an essayist, poet and dramatist and published several plays which were frequently performed at Drury Lane, Covent Garden and the Haymarket: the best known and most successful was *The Adopted Child* (1795). However, the foundation of his success lay in his business. Birch & Birch was one of the best known eating houses in London, situated opposite the Bank of England at no 15 Cornhill and especially renowned for its turtle soup and the confectionery which gained Birch the satirical nickname 'Mr Patty Pan'. He sold the business in 1836 – the year before this picture was painted – to Messrs Ring & Brymer, under whose name it evolved into a catering company that exists to this day. Birch's original shopfront is in the Museum of London.

The artist is Mary Martha Dutton, second wife of the City Solicitor Charles Pearson. She depicts Birch as Lord Mayor, despite the fact that more than twenty years had elapsed since his mayoralty. His arm rests on papers which allude to notable events during his term of office – the Duke of Wellington's victory over the French at Waterloo on June 18 1815, Napoleon's surrender, of which the news reached London on July 21, and the Corn Laws, the first of which was passed in 1815 to protect the price of home-grown grain by restricting imports of cheaper foreign grain. The measure resulted in great distress among the poor as the price of bread – a staple food – increased, leading to food riots. Birch played a

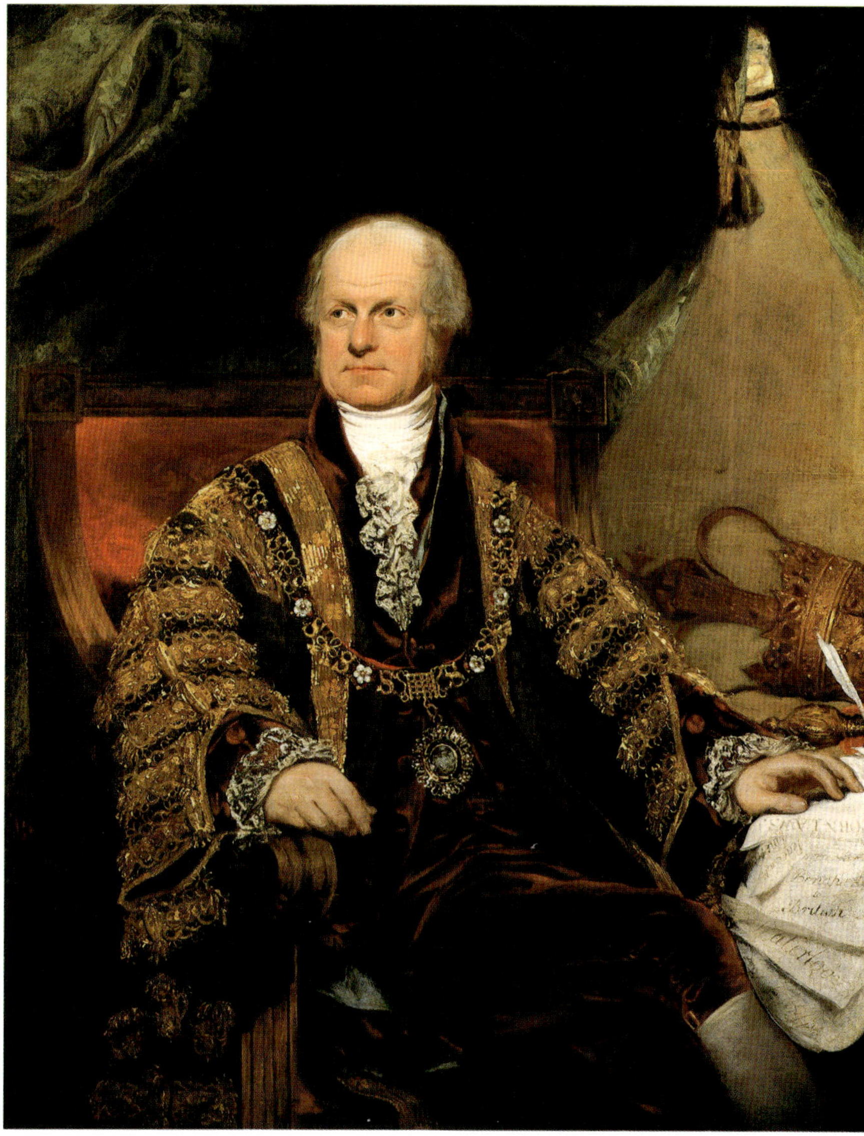

vigorous role in the City's opposition to it, probably because as a pastrycook he too would have felt the effects of higher flour prices. His opposition was commemorated by a medal struck in his honour which showed his portrait on one side with a wheatsheaf on the other with the motto 'Free Importation, Peace and Plenty'.

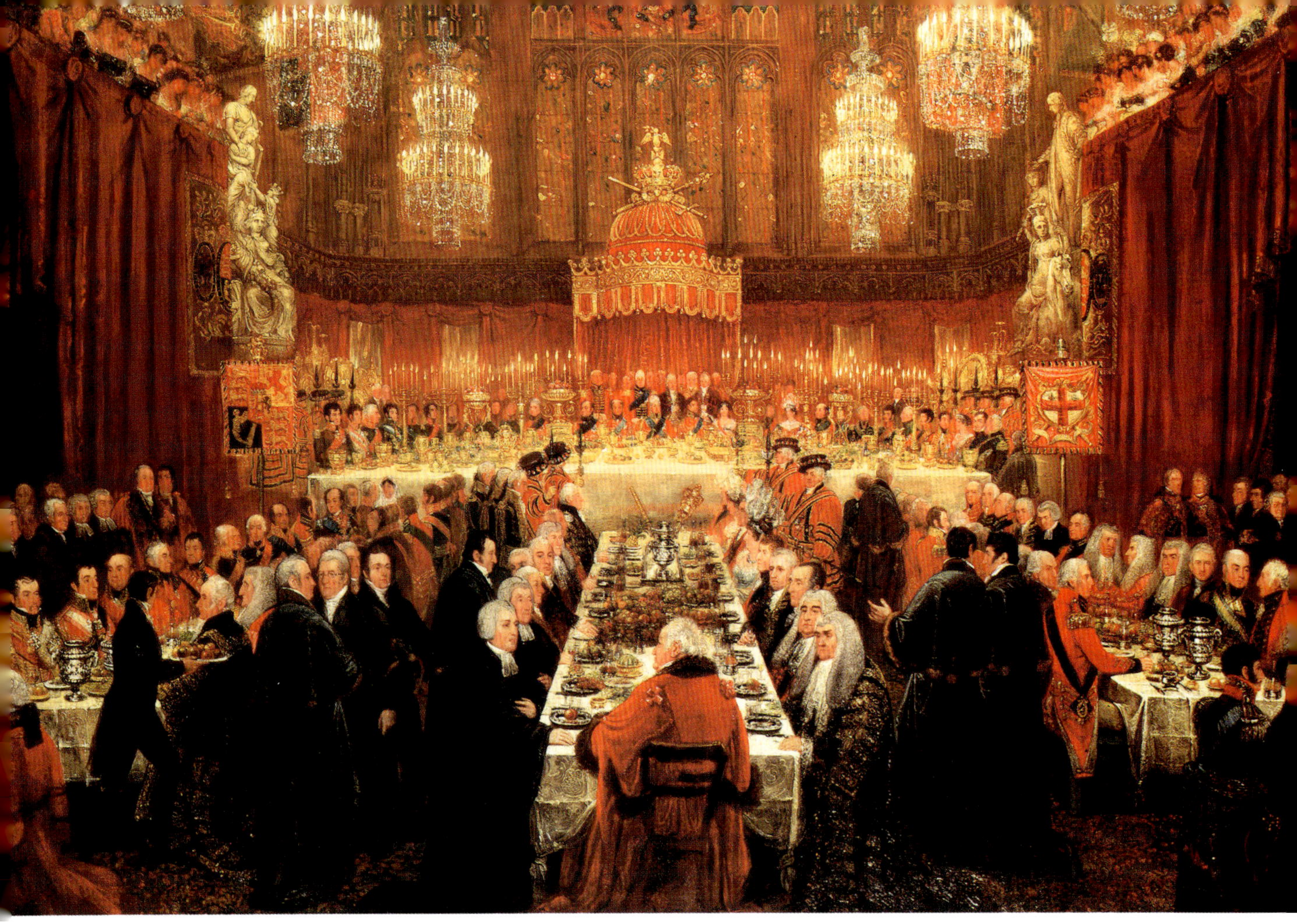

LUKE CLENNELL 1781-1840

The Allied Sovereigns Banquet at Guildhall, June 18 1814

oil on canvas

Presented by Sir William Dunn, 1923

The painting depicts the banquet held at Guildhall for the Prince Regent, Alexander I the Emperor of Russia and Frederick William III the King of Prussia, in celebration of peace with France and the end of the Napoleonic wars. The arrangements – made in only eight days – included not only the most lavish decorations but actual structural alterations to the building under the supervision of the Corporation's surveyor, George Dance. The Fishmongers' Company lent their silver chandelier to be hung over the Royal table; banners of the Livery Companies were borrowed and suspended from the roof; the banquet was served entirely off gold and silver plate and the Drapers', Goldsmiths' and Vintners' Companies lent their plate in addition to the City plate from Mansion House and that of 'several distinguished Noblemen and Gentlemen' (it was still necessary to spend more than £1000 on hiring further services; almost as much was spent on hiring additional chandeliers). On the night of the Banquet the Guildhall presented the most opulent appearance imaginable, and to enable the public to enjoy the spectacle (which had cost more than £20,000) everything was left in place for three days after the event.

The Laing Art Gallery owns a pen and ink sketch by Clennell made at the banquet while Guildhall Art Gallery also holds an impressionistic little oil sketch on copper which is believed to be by him, but it is unknown how he obtained permission to sketch in the Guildhall nor how he came to be commissioned by the 7th Earl of Bridgewater – visible in the painting seated on the right hand table – to commemorate the occasion: he may have begun the picture speculatively. A newspaper report of 1818 states that Clennell was to have painted 'another upon a very large scale' for the Corporation to hang at Guildhall; however there is no mention of this in the Corporation's records and indeed another artist – William Daniell – was commissioned to produce a small view of the banquet, which is also still in the Guildhall Art Gallery collection.

Born in Ulgham, Northumberland, Clennell had been apprenticed to the engraver Thomas Bewick. He moved to London at the end of his term in 1804 and five years later married a daughter of Charles Warren, an eminent engraver whose wide circle of artist friends included the President of the Royal Academy Benjamin West. West encouraged the young and ambitious Clennell to abandon engraving for painting, and from 1810 Clennell also worked in watercolour and oils. His observant drawings and watercolours are full of atmosphere and movement but in 1814 he was still comparatively inexperienced as an easel painter and the technique and manner of his rustic landscapes and coastal views in oil are laboured in comparison with his animated drawings. Much of this picture's surface is marked by drying cracks, showing that he laid in a dark red underpainting and painted over it before the lower layer was sufficiently dry. Obvious alterations and reworkings testify to his difficulties with the composition, and many faces are only blocked in with blank pink ovals while others are clearly defined. Those that are completed include the Duke of Wellington seated on the table at the left, Alderman and Sheriff Christopher Magnay and Rowland Hill (for which there are exact watercolour studies in the British Museum), and the Lord Mayor, Sir William Domville (a study of Domville in the British Museum was not used); Clennell himself appears as the young man in a group standing between the tables at the left. The Chamberlain, Sir James Shaw (for whom there is a study in the Royal

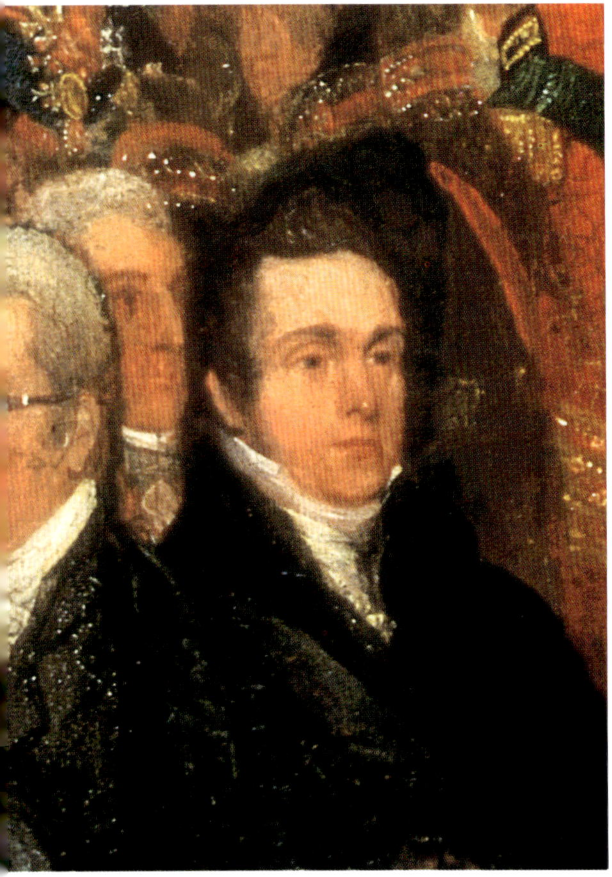

Academy) is seated near the top of the centre table next to Lady Castlereagh (Clennell told his friend Edward Willis that when sketching in the Guildhall he had accidentally thrust his stick through her dress – which Willis said was a bad omen). The place settings and the fruit on the tables are painted with the greatest attention and clarity, and sadly Clennell must have had plenty of time to concentrate on these details, for he was not sufficiently known as a painter – let alone a portrait painter – for the most important guests at the banquet to want to sit to him. Many years later it was said that 'the task of persuading the high-born to sit, the fears that some of them expressed lest their position at the table should not be important enough, or that, in other hands than those of a regular portrait painter, they would not have all the graces and courtesies of their nature limned and set in appropriate light, proved too much for a man not accustomed to meet and smooth down such difficulties'. (None of the allied dignitaries felt these concerns about the better-known and socially more adept Thomas Lawrence, who experienced no difficulty in obtaining sittings from them at his Russell Square studio.)

So that he could check on the progress of the picture, in 1816 Bridgewater had got Clennell to take a studio in Westminster at £3 a week and this must have been a considerable financial burden on the artist who lived in Islington and had three young children. He must have found the stress of being unable to get sittings while still having to meet the expense of the studio and receive the visits of his patron unbearable. His friend and fellow-engraver James Storer explained:

'In order to afford every possible facility to his undertaking he engaged apartments on the western side of the Metropolis, where he solicited to be honoured with the sittings of the nobility, and others, whose portraits were to grace his intended picture. Here he experienced so many days of solitude, anxiety and disappointment that his mental faculties became alarmingly impaired; he presented a thoughtful and dejected appearance on every return to his family, and avoided the sight of his picture, which he had already grouped and lighted to the effect desired: at length he turned it to the wall, and refused to gratify his friends with an opportunity of inspecting it'.

In April 1817 Clennell's depression culminated in a complete mental breakdown from which he never recovered. For a time he was confined in a private asylum in London, where his care may have been managed by the enlightened Dr David Uwins, brother of the artist Thomas Uwins (who had painted Clennell's wife in 1808) and physician to the Artists' Fund of which Clennell was a member, but around 1820 he was transferred to the care of Dr William Finch in Salisbury. Unusually for the period, Finch believed in regular medical attention, minimal restraint and the therapeutic effects of recreation and exercise and by 1827 Clennell was well enough to be living with a relative in Northumberland and in 1828 with his brother John, a gardener, in Newcastle. However, in 1830 he was admitted to Newcastle Lunatic Asylum, where – sometimes restrained in a straitjacket – he remained until his death, writing childlike poetry and completely unable any longer to draw or engrave. It has been suggested that he was suffering from schizophrenia which had remained latent until triggered by depression arising from his inability to complete the picture.

Elizabeth Clennell herself went out of her mind with despair and died in 1818 a few months after the death of her fourth child. A Committee of artists was formed to raise funds for the support of their three surviving children (the eldest only eight years old), and the Earl of Bridgewater agreed to take the painting even in its unfinished state (he was to have paid £1,500 for the completed picture). Some work may have been done on it by another hand, and a letter from Benjamin West to Charles Warren on 3 February 1819 names the portrait painters Thomas Phillips and William Owen as 'the two gentlemen agreed on to adjust the business between the Earl of Bridgewater and your son in law Mr Clennells [sic]'. The painting remained at Bridgewater's estate Ashridge Park and eventually passed to the 3rd Earl Brownlow. Like so many other significant pictures, it entered the Guildhall collection through the Gallery's energetic Director Sir Alfred Temple, who reported to the Library Committee in March 1923 that he personally knew the Earl's three executors and could obtain the picture – by this time misattributed to George Clint – for a nominal sum. He persuaded a former Lord Mayor, Sir William Dunn, to provide the necessary amount and a month later the purchase had been completed.

Sir George Hayter 1792-1871

Queen Victoria enthroned in the House of Lords 1838

oil on canvas

Commissioned by the Corporation, 1837

Following the eighteen-year-old Princess Victoria's accession to the throne on the death of her uncle William IV on 20 June 1837, the Recorder (Charles Laws, 1792-1850) wrote to the Lord Mayor on August 6:

'In connexion with the Queen's Visit to the City on the 9th of November I conclude the Corporation will solicit Her Majesty to sit for her Picture to be placed in or near Guildhall. I think such a proposition would very fitly emanate from you as Lord Mayor, especially as your Lordship's Mayoralty will have expired on the 9th November, altho' the Invitation to the Queen was given & accepted in your year of office. I happen to know, that Her Majesty has verbally appointed her Principal Portrait Painter Mr Hayter of Strafford Place, although the appointment is not as yet gazetted. This gentleman has executed a likeness of the Queen [his painting *HRH Princess Victoria* was exhibited at the Royal Academy in 1833] & of the Duchess of Kent – painted the celebrated Picture of the Queen's trial, & is painting the picture of the 'Reformed House of Commons' – It would I think gracefully form part of the petition to the Queen to sit for her picture – that she should do the Corporation the honour to sit for her Picture to her Principal Portrait Painter. If your Lordship should agree with me in the foregoing observations, perhaps it will also occur to you that it will be desirable to take the opportunity of the next Court of Common Council to propose from the Chair – "That her Majesty be waited upon by a deputation to request the Queen will be graciously pleased to sit for her Picture to her Principal Portrait Painter – that the Picture when finished may be placed in or near the Guildhall of the City -" It would not I think be a bad opportunity of getting rid of Queen Caroline, by making our Young Queen the pendant to the Princess Charlotte – which would have the effect of leaving the Statue of George the Third between his two gran-daughters – Charlotte & Victoria.' (The portraits of the badly-treated Queen Caroline and her daughter Princess Charlotte by James Lonsdale had been presented by Caroline in 1820 and hung in the Common Council Chamber, where the statue of George III commissioned by the Corporation from Chantrey had been installed in 1815.)

Her procession passing through streets thronged with cheering crowds, Queen Victoria's state visit took place on 9 November 1837; it was the last time that a reigning monarch has been entertained at Guildhall on Lord Mayor's Day and a painting by J H Nixon of

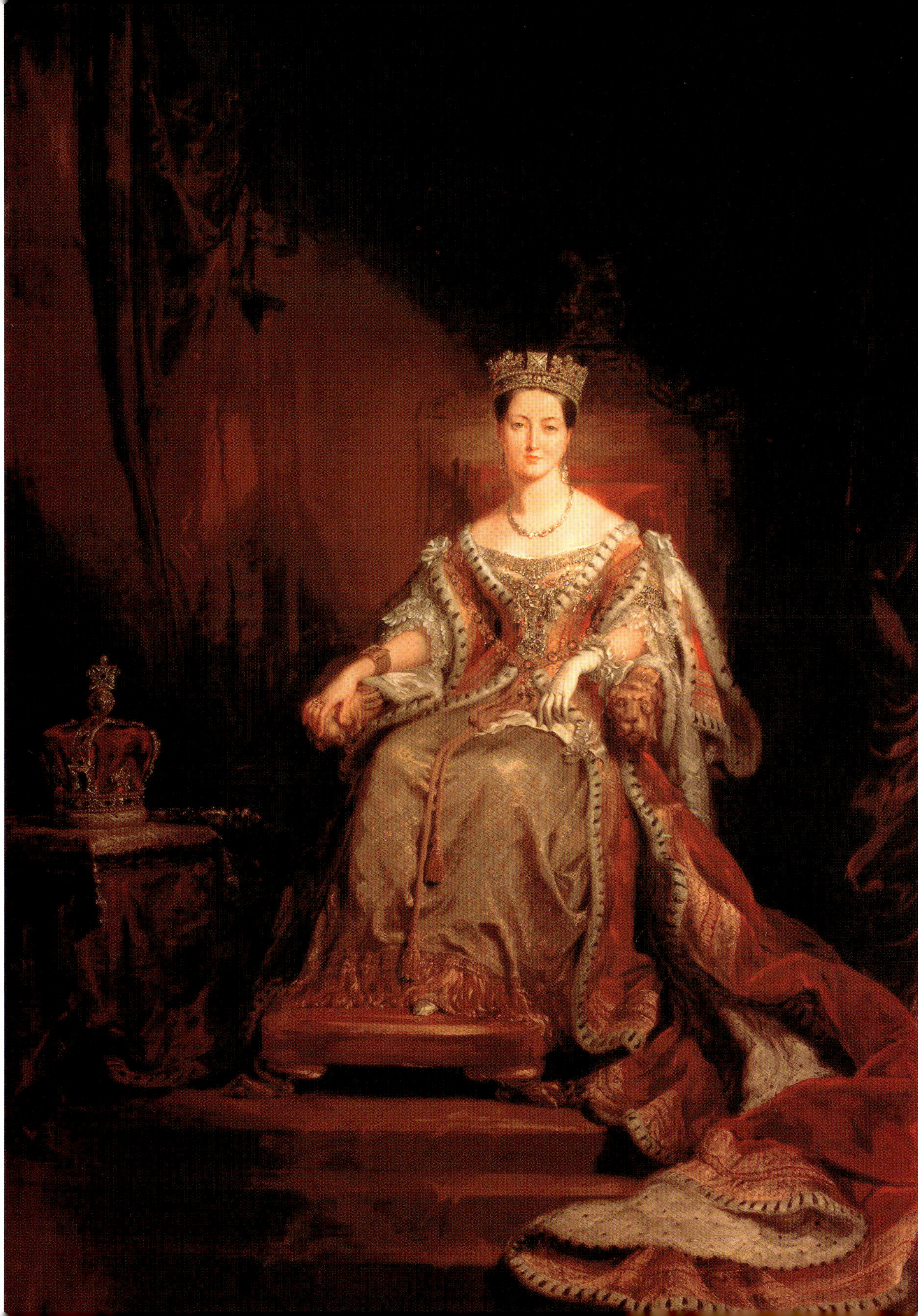

the procession passing St Paul's Cathedral is illustrated in another book in this series, *Victorian Paintings*. However it was not until 20 December that the deputation waited on the Queen and received her agreement to sit for a portrait which she said she would be pleased to present to the City. Victoria was not crowned at Westminster until June 18 1838, by which time Hayter's painting was already on exhibition at the Royal Academy with the title *Portrait of Her Most Gracious Majesty Queen Victoria, seated on the throne in the House of Lords, Painted by her Majesty's Command for the City of London*. After the Corporation received the picture it was, as Laws had suggested, hung near the statue of George III in the Common Council Chamber, but he clearly had not anticipated its size – 106 x 87 inches – which was almost twice the size of Lonsdale's portrait of Princess Charlotte and meant that it could not be paired with hers as he had envisaged.

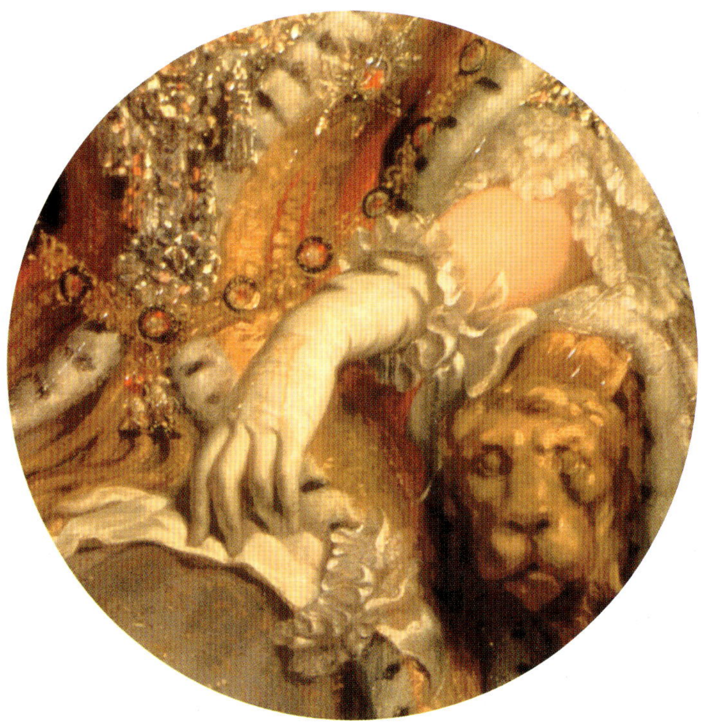

Sir John Lavery 1856-1941

Portrait of Lady Lavery (also known as *The Silver Swan* or *Hazel in Rose and Grey*)

oil on canvas
Presented by Lady Cunard, 1923

Born in Chicago, the seventeen-year old Hazel Jenner Martyn met the Belfast-born John Lavery – a widower of forty-eight with a young daughter – in 1904 while painting in Brittany. Hazel married her fiance shortly afterwards, but following his death four months after the wedding, a period of illness and the birth of her daughter, she returned to Europe and married Lavery at Brompton Oratory in 1910.

Hazel became a celebrated society hostess renowned for her beauty, and the Laverys' home in Cromwell Place was famed for her luncheons and dinner parties where painters and writers rubbed shoulders with judges and Cabinet Ministers. She developed a passionate interest and involvement in Ireland's politics, and had an affair (which was sanctioned or at least tacitly condoned by her husband) with the Sinn Fein MP Michael Collins. Hazel's position in society enabled her to act as a go-between to the politicians of opposing factions over the issue of Home Rule, and when she died in 1935 her obituarist in *The Times* explained: 'it was her untiring personality that persuaded the English ministers and the Irish leaders to exchange opinions and even to meet in her husband's studio [...]. It was in private letters to Lady Lavery that the Irish leaders were able to convey their hopes and wishes to the English Cabinet [...] In this informal manner she was able to perform a real service to the land of her adopted abode and to the country which she admired and loved.' Hazel may have helped to persuade Michael Collins to accept the treaty offered by London which led to his murder by hard-line Republicans on August 18 1922.

Michael Collins and Sir Shane Leslie had been overwhelmed by this portrait when they saw it in Lavery's studio, and Collins kept Leslie's florid description of it together with a picture of Hazel and a lock of her hair, which were found on his body after his death. Lavery exhibited this picture (together with his portrait of Collins) at the Grosvenor Gallery in July 1922 and it was bought by Hazel's friend Lady Cunard. She offered it to the Tate Gallery, but it was declined, and on October 1 1923, Sir Alfred Temple reported to the Library Committee in these terms:

'On the 2nd August last at a house in Harley Street I chanced to take up a copy of the 'Daily Mail' of that date, and in it I saw a reproduction of the picture by Sir John Lavery, R.A., which Lady Cunard has offered to the National Gallery of British Art (the Tate

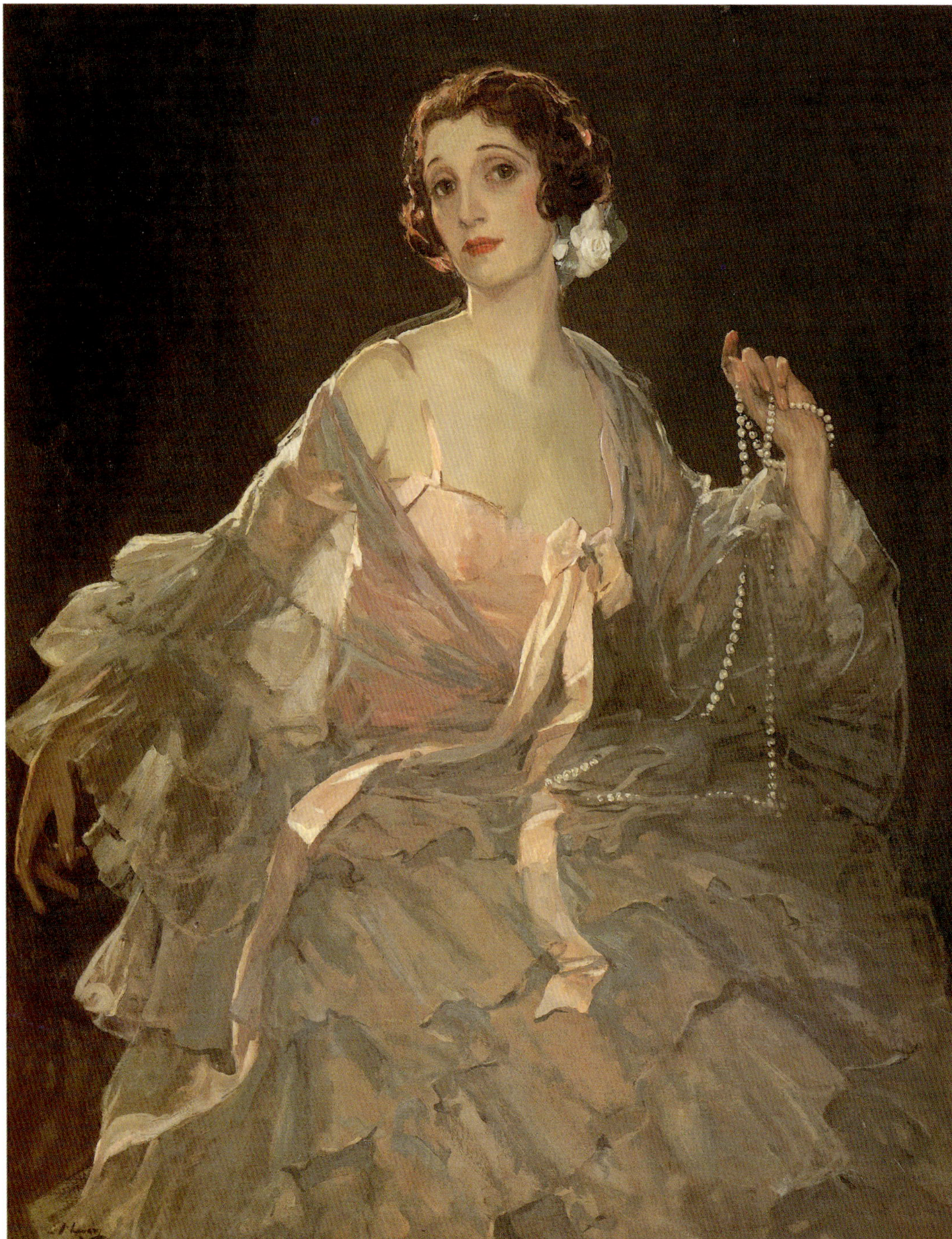

Gallery), but which the trustees of that institution had not accepted. It struck me as being a fine example of Lavery's work and I could not conjecture why the trustees of the Tate Gallery had not promptly accepted it. As soon as I was free I took a taxi to the Grosvenor Gallery where the picture was on exhibition and was so impressed with it that I went on without delay to 5 Carlton House Terrace, the residence of Lady Cunard. She had a luncheon party on, which I was invited to join, and I found all her guests to be most sympathetic with her at what they regarded as the unreasonable action of the trustees of the Tate Gallery.

I informed her I had only that day seen the picture for the first time and that I was impressed with it as a fine example of Lavery's work. Lady Cunard then asked me what action I thought she ought to take now in the matter. I therefore begged her to forgive me if I ventured to tell her what was in my mind, and I suggested that she should transfer her offer from the Tate Gallery to the Guildhall Gallery, for it was practically a national gallery, open freely to the people. The suggestion appealed to her and to all who were at the table, and the following day she came down to the Guildhall and Sir John and Lady Lavery, to whom I had telephoned to join us came also. I then learned that the Birmingham Corporation Gallery had written to her suggesting the presentation of the picture to that institution, and that the Luxembourg in Paris had expressed a strong desire to have it. We all talked together for some time in my room, when she told me in reference to my suggestion, that she felt it a little difficult to make an offer of the picture again to any public body after the course the trustees of the Tate Gallery had taken, but if I would write and inform her that my committee would like to possess the work for its permanent collection in the Guildhall, she would gladly place it at their disposal. On this I saw your Chairman, who warmly advocated my making this representation to Lady Cunard.' In his letter to her Temple noted: ' I am much gratified that any effort of mine has been instrumental in bringing permanently to the Gallery so decorative a work of John Lavery's. When the time comes he and I will act in consulation as to the position it will occupy on our walls, so that it will have the particular light most suitable for it'; Lady Cunard replied that she was pleased to let the Corporation have the painting.

After Hazel's death in 1935 Lady Cunard decided she would like to offer the portrait again to the Tate Gallery, feeling 'in view of the widespread public sympathy aroused by the death of Lady Lavery a few days ago, that the picture should be transferred to a gallery where more people would have the opportunity of seeing it – for the Guildhall Gallery has comparatively few visitors' (*Evening Standard*, January 8 1935). Lavery agreed to her suggestion that he should compensate the Gallery with another portrait of Hazel, but the Library Committee refused to give the picture up.

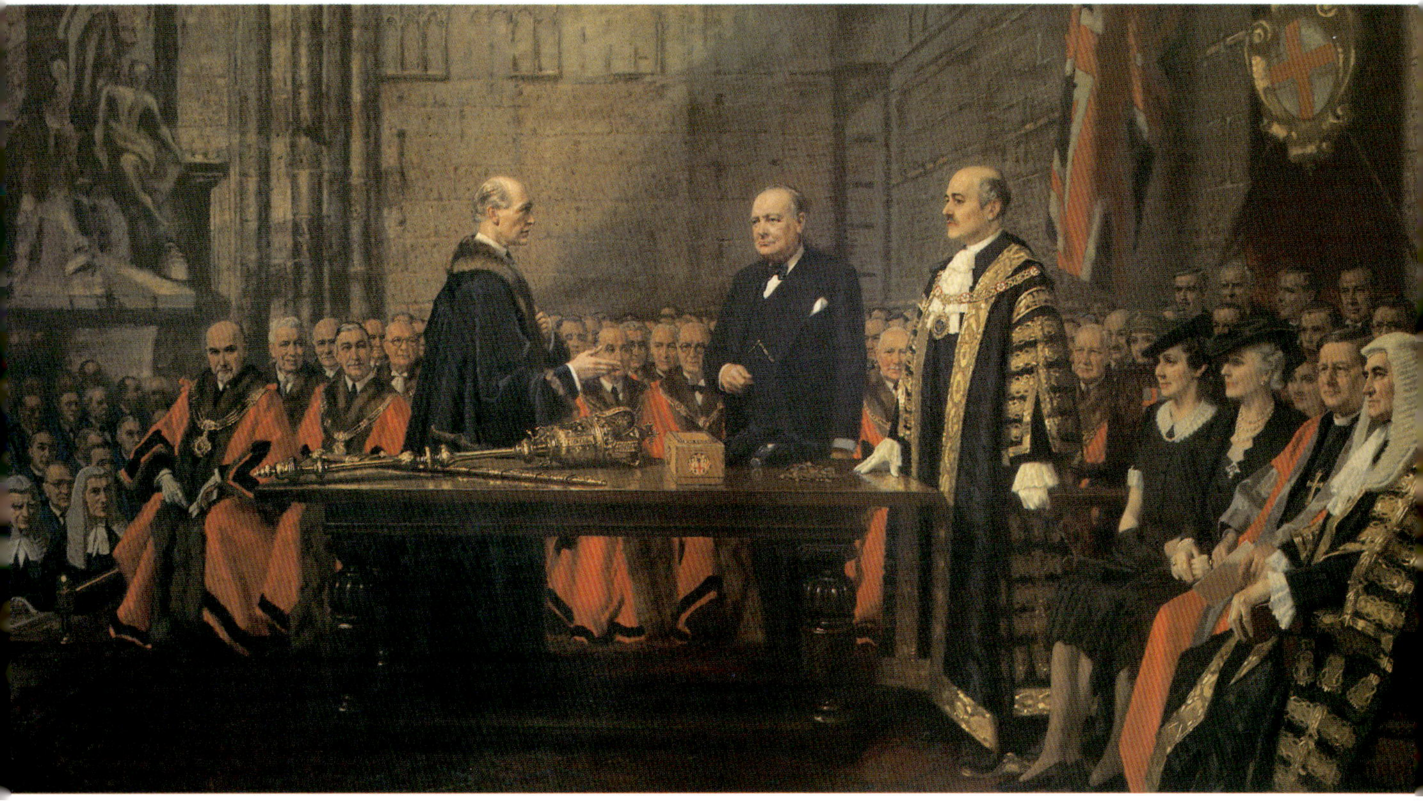

Sir Frank Salisbury

Presentation of the Freedom of the City to Winston Churchill, June 30 1943

oil on canvas

Presented by Lady Joseph and Sir Keith Joseph, 1944

On June 30 1943 the Prime Minister, Winston Churchill, was presented with the Freedom of the City at Guildhall. The ceremony which brought the nation's leader to the historic heart of the City of London had a special symbolic and emotional significance, for two and a half years earlier the Guildhall had been burnt out in the terrible air raid of December 29 1940, and the casket containing the freedom certificate was made from some of the timber from its destroyed roof. Presiding over the ceremony was the Lord Mayor, Sir Samuel Joseph, who commissioned Frank Salisbury to paint the occasion and on December 2 1943 offered the painting as a gift to the Corporation.

The ceremony took place at the East end of the Guildhall with Bacon's monument to the Earl of Chatham visible in the background. With Churchill in the centre of the painting the Chamberlain of London, Sir Adrian Pollock is seen on the left with the Lord Mayor, Sir Samuel Joseph, standing at the end of the table. On the right of the composition the distinguished guests include, from left to right Sir Louis Newton (Lord Mayor 1923-24), seen between the Lord Mayor's arm and the chairback, with Clement Atlee behind him; Mary Churchill in the Wrens cap; Lady Joseph, the Lady Mayoress, seated next to Mrs Churchill; the Archbishop of Canterbury Dr Temple; and the Lord Chancellor Lord Simon. The Foreign Secretary, Anthony Eden, is among the figures on the back row, seen on the extreme left directly above the Lady Mayoress, with Lord Woolton the Minister of Food, beside him and Herbert Morrison further along, depicted above the Lord Chancellor. The faces of Churchill's daughter and son-in-law, Mr and Mrs Duncan Sandys may be seen between Mrs Churchill and the Archbishop of Canterbury. On the left of the composition below the dais are the Common Serjeant Judge Hugh Beazeley and Judge McClure in the front row, with behind them (from the left) the Town Clerk Mr A T Roach and the Chief Commoner Captain (later Sir) George Elliston MP. The Aldermen seated behind the three central figures are, from left to right, Sir John Laurie, Sir Charles McRea, Captain Hewett, Sir Frank Bowater (Lord Mayor 1938-39), Alderman Juniper, Alderman Sir Charles Davis (Sheriff 1942-43), Sir George Broadbridge (Lord Mayor 1936-37), Sir Gerald Dodson the Recorder of London, Sir Frank Newson Smith (Lord Mayor 1943-44), Sir Percy Greenaway (Lord Mayor 1932-33), Lord Norman (d.1950) and Lord Ebbisham (Lord Mayor 1926-27). The Corporation's Coat of Arms is displayed on the extreme right, flanked by the crossed flags of the nation and the City, and the City's insignia – the Sword and Mace – lie on the table. Photographs taken of the occasion show that Salisbury omitted unpicturesque elements like microphone stands, while the table, although recognisably a piece of Guildhall furniture, was not the one actually used on that day.

Invited to be present at the historic occasion in the ancient 'badly battered and war-scarred' Guildhall, Salisbury obtained individual sittings from the distinguished individuals depicted, including Churchill, whom he had painted on several earlier occasions and this time, as the artist recorded in his autobiography Sarum Chase (1953), though very busy, gave him a sitting late one evening, coming in a car from 10 Downing Street. Salisbury went on to record that 'when completed the picture was hung with formal ceremony and presented to the Guildhall Art Gallery'. What he did not mention was the delicate problem which faced the Corporation after the picture was presented by Lady Joseph and Sir Keith Joseph (Sir Samuel Joseph having died in October 1944) in a private ceremony at Mansion House on November 30 1944. Historical inaccuracies were soon noticed, a correspondent to the *City Press* on December 15 1944 suggesting that Salisbury had taken too much liberty with the truth in painting the Chamberlain handing the casket containing the Freedom to the Prime Minister when in fact it had remained on the table throughout the ceremony, in depicting the Archbishop of Canterbury and the Lord Chancellor in robes which they had not worn and in rearranging the figures of prominent individuals. In addition, as an undated memorandum to the Library Comittee noted, 'the portrait of Sir Adrian Pollock is barely recognisable'.

On January 23 1945 the Librarian and the Chairman of the Library Committee visited the artist at his Hampstead home to discuss 'in a friendly manner' the criticisms which had been levelled against the picture. Salisbury responded that he had used artistic licence in his interpretation of the event, putting the Archbishop and Lord Chancellor in their robes to lend the picture a proper balance of colour, and grouping the figures in order to create a dramatic composition. The casket was, in his opinion, the important central feature of the painting. Nevertheless, by March 7 Sir Keith Joseph had managed to persuade the artist to make a change which, in the Committee's opinion, was 'of vital importance to the records of the City's ancient ceremonial', namely to show the Chamberlain extending the right hand of fellowship towards the Prime Minister instead of presenting the casket.

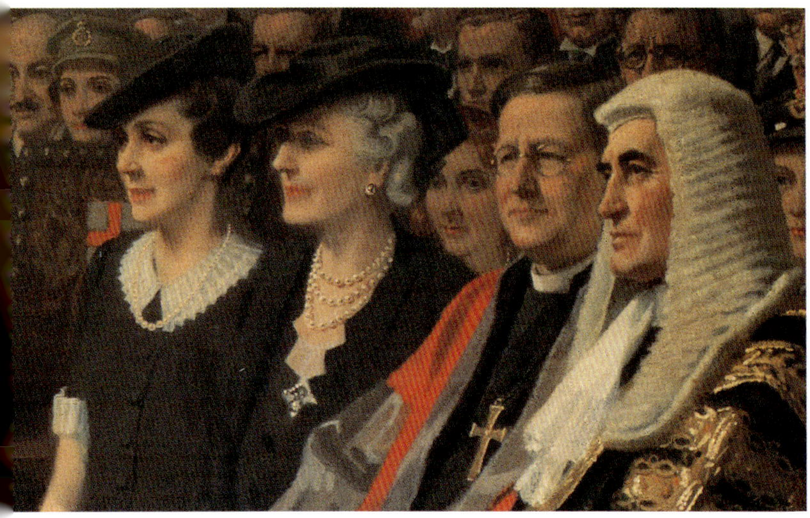

But after the painting was delivered to Salisbury's studio he changed his mind again, explaining 'While I am anxious to regard & carry out the wishes of your Committee upon very careful consideration for their point of view I now feel that your request is a great mistake, if it is a question of the letter [illegible word written over the deleted word 'destroyed'] symbolically the picture will lose its historical significance, onlookers will say Mr Churchill is evidently being made a Plymouth Brother. The picture as it is represents the historical incident. I have had the picture on the easel in progress for a whole year, 40 men and women [who] were present witnessed the ceremonial & sat to me saw the picture in progress & not one [word illegible] its representation wrong, and when the Prime Minister came to sit here the first thing he asked for in taking the pose was the box 'Give me the box' he said, That is the impression of the presentation on the mind of an infallible historian. May I ask if your Library Committee in their deliberation had the picture before them & considered the subject from this point of view.'

'I was requested by the Lord Mayor Sir Samuel Joseph to paint 'The presentation of the freedom' & he & Lady Joseph watched with keen interest its development stage by stage. so did Mr Duncan Sandys the PM's son-in-law, & the casket made of the timbers of the war damaged roof of the Guildhall was always the vital & most engaging interest to everybody.'

Two days later, on March 27th, the Chairman firmly replied: 'May I say that while I fully appreciate and sympathise with your point of view, the Committee were unanimous in accepting your kind offer [i.e. to make the required alterations]. At their meeting on the 5th instant they gave earnest consideration to the arguments put forward for your interpretation of the ceremony. They did feel strongly, however, that from the point of view of historical accuracy, the picture should be in this item, a faithful transcription of the event. May I inform you that the whole crux of the presentation of the Freedom lies precisely in the extension of the right hand of fellowship to the recipient. Perhaps this is, as you say, an ordinary gesture; but in this context it is symbolical of the reception into the body of freemen of the City of a new member. This it is, and not the handing over of the box, which gives the picture its distinction and importance from a ceremonial point of view. My Committee do feel, and I am quite certain the majority of the members of the Corporation would feel, that a gesture based on ancient tradition and with so much significance behind it should have its due regard.'

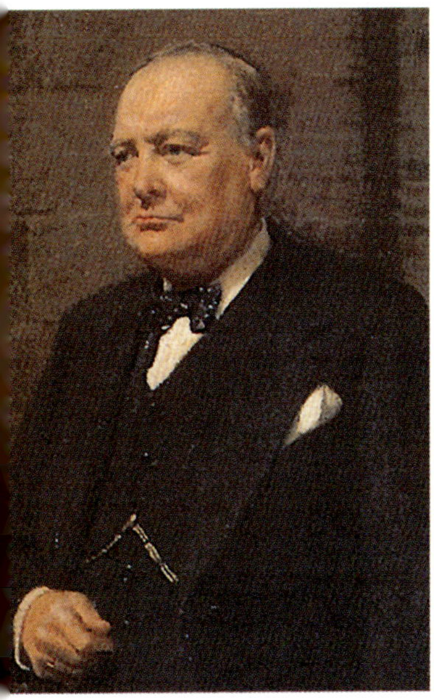

On April 18th the Chairman and the Librarian again visited Salisbury's studio and inspected the proposed alterations (by means of a drawing on cellophane placed over the painting), and after some further discussion the artist agreed to repaint the offending parts. On May 15 he wrote to the Chairman: 'I have now completed the alterations to the picture commemorating the Freedom of the City of London being conferred upon the Prime Minister. A Cabinet Minister was here last week & when he saw the picture as it is now said 'There is the sigar [sic] box on the table' I was very disappointed at this reaction. for now it is no longer the casket containing the scroll of Freedom but merely a sigar box. However that is your responsibility. The picture is now ready if you will kindly send for it.'

Perhaps Salisbury eventually concluded the changes were not as damaging as he first thought. Six years later he wrote to the Librarian that he was 'glad to have put the Churchill picture right'.

William Dring 1904-1990

Presentation of the Freedom of the City to HRH the Princess Elizabeth, June 11 1947

oil on canvas
Presented by Sir W Bracewell-Smith Bt, 1948

The Guildhall was still scarred and blackened when Princess Elizabeth came in an open carriage along a route lined with thousands of people to receive the Freedom of the City of London in 1947: the occasion had an added emotional charge in that it was the first time that a Royal Princess had accepted the Freedom. Seen standing with his back to the spectator is the Chamberlain of London, Sir Irving Cane, with the City insignia – the Sword, Mace and Cap of Maintenance – on a table beside him, while the Freedom is presented to the Princess by the Lord Mayor, Sir Bracewell Smith. (Like Salisbury, Dring omitted from the scene the microphone stand which appears on the table in photographs of the occasion.) On the left of the painting, seated from left to right in the front row are Aldermen Sir John Laurie Bt, Sir George Wilkinson Bt, Sir Frank Bowater Bt, the Rt Hon Lord Broadbridge KCVO and Lord Ebbisham CBE; while behind them sit (from left to right) Sir Keith Joseph, Sir Leslie Boyce KBE, Sir Frederick Wells, Captain RR Scott-Hewett, Septimus Marshall, Cuthbert Ackroyd and Sir Charles Davis Bt. The Recorder of London, Sir Gerald Dodson, sits behind Lord Ebbisham. Seen seated behind and to the left of the Lord Mayor is Lady Margaret Seymour. The ceremony is watched by the distinguished guests seated on the right hand side of the painting, including, from right to left, the Prime Minister Clement Attlee and Mrs Attlee, The Rt Hon Lord Jowett (the Lord Chancellor) and Lady Jowett, the Archbishop of Canterbury, HRH the Princess Margaret, Lady Bracewell-Smith and Sir Andrew Duncan.

Archive photographs of the occasion correspond closely with the composition of the picture, and like Clennell more than a century earlier the artist evidently laid this out first (in this case using one or more photographs for reference) before obtaining sittings from the individuals involved, whom he drew in the required poses. Guildhall Art Gallery purchased fourteen of his detailed and highly finished pastel studies for the individual portraits in this painting from the artist in 1988.

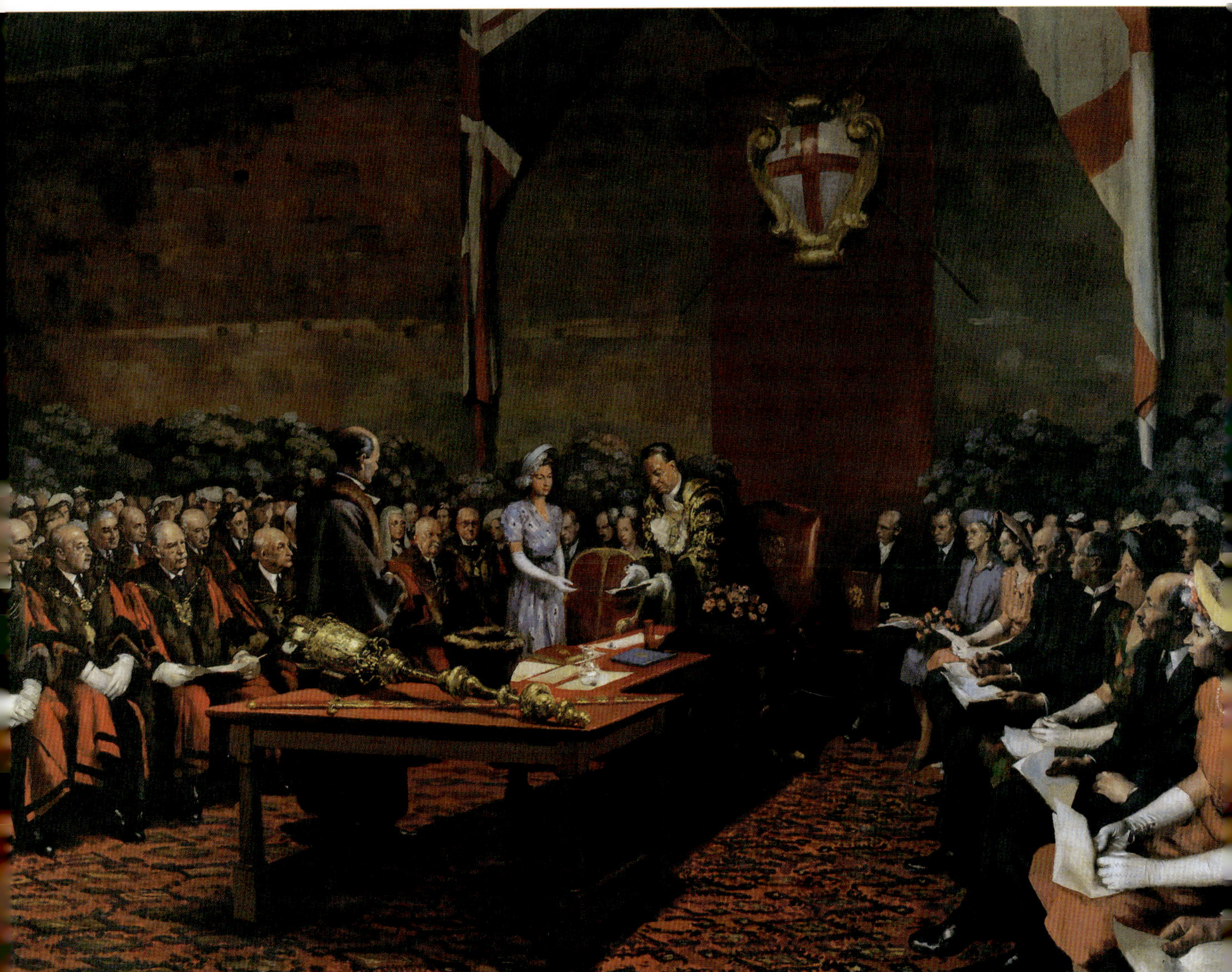

Index of Artists

Index of Subjects